The Dracula Spectacula

The Dracula Spectacula

Book and Lyrics by
John Gardiner

Music by
Andrew Parr

Samuel French – London
New York – Sydney – Toronto – Hollywood

ISBN 0 573 18013 X

The Vocal Score for this play is available from Samuel French Ltd

Printed in Great Britain by
Biddles Ltd, Guildford, Surrey

THE DRACULA SPECTACULA

or

'Fangs ain't what they used to be'

CAST

MISS NADIA NAIVE	a sweet, vulnerable American schoolteacher
MARVIN or KELLY	an insatiable appetite for popcorn
LUKE or JULIE	an intellectual with freckles and glasses
ELVIS	could it really be him?

Transylvanian Airways PILOT
Pretty SINGERS
Transylvanian Airways DANCERS

MASTER LANDAU   a coachdriver

The OUT-PATIENTS of Karloffia Sanatorium for Glublick Addicts on day release:

CLOD	RAFF
LOOBY	BOGIE
SCRUB	BOOTS
SCRATCH	DREGS
RIFF	BOOZE

The Glublick Welly Boot DANCERS

HERR HANS	a Transylvanian innkeeper
FRAU GRETEL	his wife

PROFESSOR NICHOLAS
  NECROPHILIAC   a young English doctor with a mission

FATHER O'STAKE   a good Irish priest

The BRIDES of Count Dracula

The ZOMBIE MEN

The COUNT DRACULA

The COUNTESS WRAITH	his lunatic mother
GENGHIS	his crook-backed retainer

SCENES

Scenes will take place in a small classroom, on a big aeroplane, on a stony road, in a cosy inn, at a table, on two chairs, in a dark castle, up the North Tower, on an open piece of countryside, in a nasty dungeon, in the Castle crypt, back at the inn, and inside your mind.

NOTES ON THE PLAY

PRESENTATION

The musical was originally evolved for secondary school pupils but the piece will work just as well with an adult group. The musical is such that it can either cater for large numbers or by doubling or trebling up become a very satisfying 'ensemble' or 'group theatre' vehicle. The comedy of the situation would probably be heightened by such a treatment. The main problem of writing for children is finding an attractive vehicle, which caters for large numbers, which allows them to use a wide range of allied theatre arts (mask, design, dance, etc.), and which allows for inventive improvisation so that the eventual production is very much 'their' show. We think that THE DRACULA SPECTACULA SHOW has such qualities.

Each character affords the opportunity to play both 'comedy' and 'melodrama' and as such both themes should be played with expertise. Those moments which are atmospheric should be played with sensitivity and total belief, no matter how far fetched the fantasy. In no circumstances should these serious moments in the musical be allied to the 'sending up' or 'spoof' sequences. These abrupt changes of mood can, of course, be heightened by the use of light, music and sound effects. The musical can be staged in any manner, although it does help to have space. The scenery needs to be set and struck at speed and you will find that the Village Idiots make an ideal stage crew. Details of the original set used may be found under 'Scenery and business'.

The band can be placed above the performers (we suggest the kind of scaffold tower used by caretakers to clean down the ceilings). It is also advisable to use microphones simply because some of the numbers require a hard square, loud rock sound and others the intimacy of the breathy nightclub singer. The microphones can be planted into the most unlikely stage props and used as part of the general business, eg: NADIA's hand mirror, a bottle of Glublick, the top of the Stake, etc. The make-up of the band can be left to personal preference but you will probably find that an organ is a fairly versatile, spooky instrument and the original production featured a piano, lead guitar, bass guitar and percussion.

DRACULA and the VAMPIRES, although they are gaudy figures, should still retain a sinister quality. DR NICHOLAS should be a clean-cut, handsome, totally dependable hero throughout and his honesty of purpose not one jot less attractive than NADIA's dumb-blonde ingenue. The PUPILS' dialogue will rapidly go out of fashion, as will a few of the 'running gags' like the life-force substitute 'Pepsi-Cola' - so directors should be alert to 'in' alternatives and must feel quite free to weave their own topical material into the fabric of the show. The VILLAGE IDIOTS'

success depends upon careful grouping and although they have little
actual dialogue they can in fact steal the show - we see them as a cross
between Snow White's dwarfs and the rabble from the 'Threepenny Opera'.
They have all been given idiosyncratic names and the players should use
their imaginations as to how best these may be developed. Both GENGHIS
and COUNTESS WRAITH are merely tools of the COUNT and as with most
misused fools they should evoke the pity of the audience, they are not
horrific creatures. FATHER O'STAKE is no fool, however, and he should
use his Irish descendancy and blarney, as a setter of scenes and a teller
of stories.

MONEY

Extra money may be made by selling the posters that advertise the show,
groups or schools might like to record cassettes of their production to
sell at exorbitant prices. The tickets may be designed like bats, and
novel programmes sold by homuncules in the auditorium. There is at
present on the market a Dracula ice-lolly and you could also include 'life
force substitute' on your list of confections for sale. A prize could be
offered to that member of the audience at any performance who supplies
the worst horror 'pun' of the run. Supply a board where they can write
their attempt plus their addresses. In fact making the audience know they
are going to enjoy the show before it starts is an important presentation
factor. 'Follow the ghouls' footmarks' for the entrance to the auditorium,
block out the original door into the shape of a coffin lid with handles,
that creaks as you enter auditorium. Have fun on these lines. There is
so much you can do, from give-away badges to stick-on patches.

COSTUMES

The musical can be dressed in period costume à la Carpathia and any
good gothic novel will provide illustrations. There are on sale also
selections of horror film stills with the range stretching from 'The
Cabinet of Dr Caligari' to Hammer's 'Dracula, Prince of Darkness'.
We decided in the original production to choose very modern clothes for
the Americans, mainly because it kept costs down and allowed a wider
range of opportunity when it came to caricature and comedy.

1. DRACULA was dressed in a Lugosi dress suit for the first half, with
a black high collared cloak. In the second half he changes into an
outrageous silver glitter suit, high stilted silver boots, silver eye make-
up and white face, carmined purple lips and purple eye line.

2. GENGHIS can be dressed in all black motor-cycle leathers with a
German Stormtroopers helmet (black) plus the usual trappings of
swastikas, silver chains, gauntlets, and skull and crossbones on the
jacket back. The hunch is a simple strapped pillow. Or dressed in the
authentic black coat and tails, diseased face and bandaged fingers and

covered in talcum powder dust.

3. WRAITH we dressed in rags and green-grey weeds. A scatty wig, all over the place. Basic colours green and purple.

4. THE GLUBLICK ADDICTS were dressed in hospital operating gowns with operating theatre hats. The gowns were clearly numbered like convicts. Their faces displayed unsuccessful operation experiments and they wore large 'welly boots'.

5. NADIA and the PUPILS were dressed in their own latest 'with it' gear, but we insisted that the colours were subtle and gentle. Sweetness was the key note. It is not necessary that NADIA looks like Monroe nor that she is a blonde - but we think she should be pretty and wide-eyed. JULIE should have freckles around her nose, and wear heavy studious-looking glasses. KELLY carries popcorn around throughout the show, should be tubby and, if anything, a little gawky in a tomboy way. ELVIS should amble, be loose jointed, and have long sideburns plus a hair style reminiscent of Elvis Presley in his early days. (See contemporary photos.) In the original, NADIA wore a black velvet suit, high heeled boots, a white blouse and a bubble Afro wig (bright red/orange). The PUPILS wore basket ball boots, bright patch jeans and U.S.A. college vests. The PUPILS can be played alternatively as boys.

6. FATHER O'STAKE in a simple brown cassock (and sandals) but no need for a tonsure. Keep him straight.

7. DR NICK is young and good-looking and was dressed in a white suit with white shoes and tie, but a navy shirt. As the play becomes active in the Castle of the Black Lake he could change to fashionable 'mod' trousers and a white roll-necked pullover. He should be like a modern crusader.

8. HANS and GRETEL need plain rustic costumes to match their home cooking and rosy cheeks.

9. LANDAU, the coachman, a dark cloak and hat with wide brim - like an anarchist who has a smoking 'molotov cocktail' in his pocket.

10. The AIRWAY costumes will probably have to be borrowed or hired, or make some kind of special mock up uniform for 'Transylvanian Airways'. A kind of 'Star Trek' styled outfit made from coloured leotards and tights, plus a symbol ensignia - a bat wing like British Rail. 'Fly Transylvania - No return flights.'

11. THE BRIDES OF DRACULA can be dressed in full length (nylon, preferably, because it clings) nightdresses, coloured tights, violent-coloured wigs with hair spread wildly in 'Afro' style, make-up to match. The colours we envisaged were emerald green, bright orange, black, white and Prussian blue. The wigs may be supplied by a kindly local

firm, if not, hire them. It is worth spending money on these characters. Many of the girls will have wigs like this anyway, or you can paint old unwanted wigs. Designs painted directly on to feet and arms are effective – snakes, monsters of the deep, insects, etc. In the original show they wore red or black nylon negligées and wigs made of rolled silver paper stapled onto hairnets. They cost about 8p each. Similar plain white paper curled wigs were used for Act II reprise.

12.   The ZOMBIES need to be dressed in shredded clothes. Coats, trousers or shirts torn to shreds, the costumes need to be wetted and rolled in mud before each performance. They should appear as if they have just recently dragged themselves out of marsh, quicksands or very damp coffins. Huge head masks or else plain 'phantom of the opera' masks should be worn, or make up faces with Max Factor C.T.V. Clown White Pancake.

13.   The TRANSYLVANIAN DANCERS were dressed in exotic travelling gear – filmstars, etc. en route for romantic places and the dance reflected this fantasy trip.

CUTS

If running time needs to be reduced, there are two optional numbers: No. 8 'Be Silent and Attentive' and No. 36 'I'm a Nice Little Girl'.

SCENERY AND BUSINESS

This is only a guide as to how the musical can be staged. In the original production the stage allowed for most of the signs and tricks to be flown from the grid, but, if this is not possible, use falling flaps, reversible flats or rotating gravestones. These signs could become very comic additions to the general business.

The performing area was divided into five playing areas:
    (a)   the main central playing area
    (b)   the graveyard and mausoleum
    (c)   and (d)   extending catwalks stage R. and L.
    (e)   a central well between catwalks.

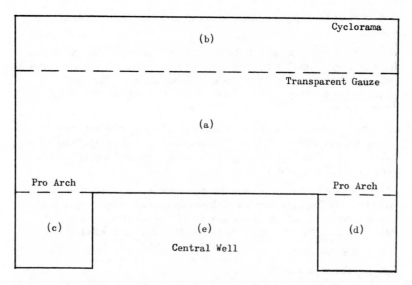

The graveyard (a) was made up of broken crosses and gothic angels, with a mausoleum C.L. on which is displayed the open coffin containing DRACULA. A candle burns at the head of the silk-lined sarcophagus. The graveyard is divided from the central playing area (b) by a white gauze. The white gauze has two advantages (i) lit from behind it creates the dreamlike/ethereal quality required for the graveyard scenes and (ii) slides from 'horror comics' can be projected on to the screen. We have not listed the slides which we originally used but there were fifty in all and they were very effective in heightening both suspense and comedy. Individual directors may choose their own pictures and the timing of projection, but because of the technical problems of projection it may be dispensed with and not detract from the show. It is very much a luxury if you can afford it.

A white gauze can be hired reasonably inexpensively from:

> 'Rex Howard',
> Metrostore,
> 231 The Vale,
> Uxbridge Road,
> London W1 7QS   Tel: 01-749 2958

The two catwalks can extend as far as space will allow and should be lit with coloured footlights like fairground signs. If you cannot extend, then space the two raised areas (c) and (d) on to the stage area (b) on either side of the stage.

The 'central well' (e) may be used for the aeroplane sequence and the chairs placed there permanently – it can also be used for a fourth dancing area.

The North Tower was a scaffolding tower on wheels, the Black Lake a normal stage trap; but if again this is not available you can use a kind of 'Sweeney Todd' false front to the Mausoleum through which the characters can disappear in a flash or simply a raised tomb that has a false trap top.

All other scenery should be very simple but bold and bright and very easily set and struck. It is a good idea to employ stage hands in three groups: (1) to set and strike on main stage area; (2) and (3) to set and strike catwalks (c) and (d).

There is a great deal of smoke and mist used in the production and if you wish to avoid the usual dry ice problems may we strongly recommend the use of a smoke machine. They are easily manoeuvred and can give extraordinary effects. An excellent machine can be hired from:

> **Richard Dendy**
>
> **2 Aultone Yard**
>
> **Aultone Way**
>
> **Carshalton, Surrey**   **Tel: 01-647 8765**

Most small hand-props are very easily acquired. The Glublick bottles are simple glass painted over to give an ageing effect, while the fake hands of GENGHIS were made from a simple plaster mould – make quite a few because they disintegrate delightfully in the 'Life Blood Substitute Laboratory'.

LIGHTING

As well as a general lighting design we used two 2000-watt follow spots for principals, a U.V. lamp for opening of Act Two, plus cloud effects 252 lamp for 'Transylvania Airways' and 'Starry Spheres'. You can use really as many effects as finances will allow but with some imagination it can be done very cheaply. Remember that gothic horror is best lit from the side and at times from below for the best spooky effects. We projected with a simple Kodak Carousel slide projector. We also lit the trap from below with a variety of colours to heighten the grotesqueness of the smoke pouring up.

THE DRACULA SPECTACULA SHOW

ACT ONE

MUSIC CUE 1

The stage is empty, no curtain, an image of DRACULA is thrown onto the screen. House lights fade. There are building sinister chords or continuous pulsing sounds which increase in intensity and are interspersed with owl hoots, flapping wings, creaking lids, nails scratching. Finally a clap of thunder and an echoing scream –

The **COMPANY** appear (hands showing first). They appear to be emerging from the very earth itself. The whole piece builds in volume and power until the final four lines which will be sung in the style of a pagan Gregorian chant. The emergence should be slow as if dragging themselves from a quicksand. The whole **COMPANY** are involved on numerous levels. Their entrances should be as varied as possible. The **COMPANY** wear full length hooded gowns, rubber gloves, white faces and white feet.

SONG: THE DRACULA SPECTACULA SHOW

LOOK! READ! GASP! QUIVER!
He's waiting for you there
GIRL MEETS! GHOUL! SHIVER!
In his castle lair.

So if you feel cosy
With Bela Lugosi
This is the show for you
There are no tomorrows
In this chamber of horrors
Check your heartrate - do.

Who is it drinks from the coffin's cup?
What goes down, but must come up?
The Prince of Vampires, The King of Night.
It's the Dracula Spectacula
The Dracula Spectacula
The Dracula Spectacula Show.

BATS! SCREECH! BLOOD! RITES!
You'll need the exorcise
WHITE! FANGS! EYES! ICE!
Do not trust that smile.

So if your cuppa tea
Could be Christopher Lee
Then fly with us tonight!
'Cos it's a two-way trip
In a cataleptic fit
Watch out in case he bites!

Who is it drinks from the coffin's cup?
What goes down, but must come up?
The Prince of Vampires, The King of Night.
It's the Dracula Spectacula
The Dracula Spectacula
The Dracula Spectacula Show!

(COMPANY collapse in broken shapes over area.
Follow spot picks up FATHER O'STAKE who holds
 a candle and addresses towards DRACULA,
revealed behind gauze.)

O'STAKE   (spotlighted high)   Dracula, in life you did one
deed which at once cast you out from all hope.
You poisoned the pure font of mercy and not upon
such as you can the downy freshness of Heaven's
bounty fall! Live henceforth a being accursed!

(COMPANY move a part of the body and emit a
sound, staccato fashion, after the word 'accursed'.)

Armed against all men and all men armed against
thee!

MUSIC CUE 2

COMPANY

OF GIANT STRENGTH AND GIANT TREAD
HE SEEKS A LIFE FORCE FROM THE DEAD
SLEEPS ALL DAY, BUT WORKS ALL NIGHT
DRACULA! ECTOPLASMIC DYNAMITE!

(During the chant, the COMPANY slowly unwind
and start to move off the area in a kind of trance.
When the first bell tolls the COMPANY freeze and
FATHER O'STAKE comes from behind gauze to C.
After third toll COMPANY disappear pointing
inwards at the PRIEST.

A bright light -- a green and yellow 'gobbo' - comes
up on interior of School Room, and a slide of
American school room exterior on gauze. The
pupils, JULIE, KELLY and ELVIS enter and sit at
desks. From grid L. there is displayed a map of
Europe. The countries are painted in national
colours with symbols on each to represent
character of individual country.)

MUSIC CUE 3

O'STAKE

(from above)   Our story begins when the times
changed all things, 'tempora et omnia mutantur'.
(He admires his intelligence but realizing that the
audience is not in the slightest way impressed, he
continues in a less flippant vein.)   Imagine, if
you will, this small classroom in the United States
of America.

(He points. Lights up L.)

It is a bright sunlit day, birdsong can be heard in
the field outside

(Sound of birdsong.)

and a sweet but vulnerable young schoolteacher is
introducing her class to the mysteries of world
geography.

(Lights come up on the classroom as MISS NADIA
NAIVE enters. The PUPILS stand. The teacher is

decidedly pretty, dumb in an attractive kind of way,
and she speaks like Marilyn Monroe or any other
breathless sex symbol you may like to identify her
with.)

MISS NADIA   Please stand.

(PUPILS sit.)

Why, that's just fine. Well, children, here we are
in this small classroom somewhere in the United
States of America. It is a bright sunlit day, birdsong can be heard in the field outside

(Birdsong – but to the tune of the 'Stars and
Stripes'.)

and I, your sweet but vulnerable young schoolteacher, am introducing you to the miseries of
world geometry –   (She pauses, realising an
error but the correct word dawns on her.)
Geography.   (She smiles a 'See I can do it when
I try' sort of smile.)

PUPILS   Wow!   (Out front with a simultaneous sway of the
head towards the audience and softly incredulous.)

MISS NADIA   Now have your notebooks ready 'cos I tend to get
carried away.

(They open books with pens poised.)

Are you ready?

PUPILS   (in unison out front, like Laurel and Hardy)
Hmm.   Mmm.   Sure are.

MISS NADIA   (turning to blackboard map)   Fine. This here-
ya is Eu-rope   (She plonks an indiscriminate
mark somewhere on the map.)   and this
here-ya is the Med-iterranean Ocean.   (She has
difficulty saying it.)

PUPILS   (out front with head sweep)   Wow!   (Soft
again.)

MISS NADIA   (exhausted)   Well, that concludes world
geography for today. Any more questions?

JULIE   (studious, freckled and wearing intellectual

	glasses) Miss Naive. Whereabouts in Europe did you point? I mean which country in Eu-rope?
MISS NADIA	(confused) Where? Well, let's see. (She produces a large magnifying glass which has printed already on the lens, 'Transylvania'. She holds it up close to the mark on the map.) Why, that is France.
JULIE	Transylvania. (Correcting her with air of mechanical and bored efficiency.)
MISS NADIA	(without turning a hair) That is Transylvania.
KELLY	(a sweet girl, likeable, who stuffs herself full of candy all through the play) Miss, could we go there tomorrow (Out front and in one breath of speech as if learnt specially for the occasion.) - when our European educational vacation conveniently arranged to fit in with the plot of the play - (Breath.) commences?
MISS NADIA	Would you like to go right now?
JULIE	(taking off glasses in an executive manner) Sure would!
KELLY	(popping in a handful of gooeys) Scrummy!
ELVIS	(he talks like his namesake, chews gum, mouth droops open all the time, and speaks in a surprisingly deep blue) I like it. (To audience.) You know what I mean?
MISS NADIA	Have you got all your things packed ready? (They produce from desks, air bags marked 'Transylvanian Airways' and plonk them on desks with individual answer.)
JULIE	Sure!
KELLY	Scrummy!
ELVIS	Crazy man!
MISS NADIA	Then we shall leave immediately, travelling by air, sea and train enjoying the comfort of a first class service, delightful cuisine and a friendly smile from your tour operator - I learnt that from the brochure. (She is proud.)

PUPILS

(out front)   Yuk!

(MISS NADIA produces a vanity bag from behind the
blackboard. Map flies and desks are struck.
NADIA leads pupils to catwalk R. where aeroplane
is set. She tidies their clothing and they dance as
well as, but not with, AIRWAYS STAFF.)

MUSIC CUE 4

AIRPORT
ANNOUNCER

All passengers for Transylvanian Airways flight to
Europe please report to boarding barrier 27.

SONG: FLY TRANSYLVANIAN AIRWAYS

(A large sign marked 'BARRIER 27' appears from
above or is placed. Five white chairs are placed
catwalk R. representing the plane. Airport
OFFICIALS appear. The PILOT, who swigs from a
gigantic bottle of scotch labelled 'High Octane Fuel',
climbs into the front chair of the imaginary aircraft.
An OFFICIAL stamps the party's visas at end of
song. A CUSTOMS MAN checks their baggage and
chalks it, and two AIR HOSTESSES dance to the
plane and help them. The following movement
section is to be performed in a balletic manner but
fairly tight and slick; the group move in a
staccato-like manner, the HOSTESSES have more
dreamy flowing movements. The ballet is danced
by PASSENGERS and AIRPORT CLIENTELE. The
song is to be sung like a Martini Commercial, very
breathy and cool. It's sung by three pretty GIRL
SINGERS and two gigolo type young MEN with
Italian sideboards and droopy moustaches. They
sing, the MEN accompany with appropriate
'Oo-ah's'. The arrangement of this to be left to
individual musical directors as the 'scene' changes
year by year. So play it all according to the fashion
that is contemporary - although the score can be
taken as a firm basis or, if you trust us, as it
stands.)

Come fly Transylvanian
Fly, fly, fly,
Come fly over Pennsylvania
Fly, fly, fly.

Come fly,
Transylvanian Airways.

MEN   (speaking)   It's so easeeeeee.

Come fly Transylvanian
Fly, fly, fly,
Come fly over Yugoslavia
Fly, fly, fly.
Come fly,
Transylvanian Airways.

MEN   (speaking)   It's fantasticaaaaaaa.

Time and the world are ever in flight
So the poet says
Come fly with us to the highest height
Wrapped in clouds and snow
Just smile on those below.

Come fly Transylvanian
Fly, fly, fly,
Come fly over Transylvania
Fly, fly, fly.
Come fly,
Transylvanian Airways.

MEN   (speaking)   It's fantasticaaaaaaa.

AIRPORT   Flight 675 for Europe is now ready for take off.
ANNOUNCER   This flight stops at Paris, Heidelberg and
             Karloffia, Transylvania. Bon voyage. Goodbye.
             Auf wiedersehen. Don't say we didn't warn you.

             (All exit to busy airport-music. Then a blue light
             spots the interior of the aeroplane. The engines
             rev up. The PILOT has one more stiffening swig
             from his bottle. He is stoned.)

PILOT   This is your silot peaking. Please basten your
             safety felts, and no playing billy suggers! Here we
             go! Wheee!

             (The engines roar as for take off. The HOSTESSES
             pull back the PILOT's chair, the PASSENGERS
             lean back, simulating the rising of the aircraft.
             At the height of the engine roar, all PASSENGERS
             scream. BLACKOUT.

MUSIC CUE 5

When the light comes up, the PASSENGERS are
strewn about, but the HOSTESSES and PILOT are
wearing party hats and blowing party squeaker
blowouts. The PILOT is flying the plane with his
feet. The paraphernalia are secreted in boxes
attached to U.S. side of chairs.
The flight lasts only a short while, there is a
REPRISE of the verses 3 and 4 of COME FLY
TRANSYLVANIAN quietly under the dialogue.)

PILOT   We are now flying at a height of three thousand
                       feet, conditions are perfect –

                       (There is a clap of thunder and the occupants shake.)

                       conditions are nearly perfect and we are directly
                       over the Atlantic Ocean – I think.

PASSENGERS   (looking down at the sea on audience side)   Hi
                       there! Look at that blue! Wow! etc.

                       (They wave and peer, take snapshots, wipe the
                       porthole clear. They are excited. Then the lights
                       fade out fractionally. When they come up the
                       occupants and the PILOT are all fast asleep,
                       leaning at 45 degrees to port. The intercom wakes
                       them and they sit bolt upright as the PILOT levels
                       out the flight course.)

INTERCOM   (sinister voice)   This is Karloffia Airport,
                       Transylvania. Are you receiving me? Are you
                       receiving me? Over!

PILOT   (suddenly coming out of a dream)   I'm innocent,
                       I tell you. I never touched her. I thought she was
                       over sixteen. Innocent – What! Where?
                       (Comes to.)   Oh, sorry about that – Hello,
                       Karloffia. This is flight 675 from Pennsylvania.
                       Can you give me landing clearance? Heavy mist all
                       round up here.

INTERCOM   Flight 675. Conditions normal. There is always
                       heavy mist in Transylvania. You have landing
                       clearance for runway two. Over and out.

PILOT   Right you are. Here we go. Wheels down. Tally

ho. Oh, my God, the wheels have stuck again.
(He flicks to intercom.)   Hello, this is your
pilot speaking. We have a little trouble up here.
The wheels have jammed so we would appreciate
it if all passengers would run as quickly as possible
as soon as we touch down. It just eases the
situation. I think you'll find this a lot of fun.

HOSTESS 1   (spoken like starlets auditioning very badly)
Oh, Dolores, not again. Have you got the landing
shoes?

HOSTESS 2   Sure. Good thing too. I wore my new black shoes
completely out landing at Milan with this lunatic.

BOTH   (together, out front)   Watch out, here we go!

(The PASSENGERS watch this performance as
HOSTESSES put on wellies and as the plane comes
down with a skid they all run as if their feet are
sticking out of the bottom of the plane and slow it
down. They then collapse backwards exhausted in
their chairs.)

MUSIC CUE 6

PILOT   Well, you did just fine. Just fine. Anybody for
drinkies? See you all in the bar later maybe.
Tally-ho.

(He jumps out of plane with arms round
HOSTESSES and disappears off to an offstage riot
of piano playing and glasses clinking. He opens an
imaginary door, they all cheer. He re-opens door
with noise to say:)

Oh, by the way, have a nice stay in Transylvania.
Personally we never go further inland than this, you
know. Funny place, Transo.   (Slams the door.)

(PUPILS and MISS NADIA are left standing alone on
the stage. A wind springs up and a little fog seeps
onto the stage – darkens. They huddle into a tight
group by the pro arch R.)

JULIE   Please, Miss. How do we get to the inn?   (Looks
at map.)

ELVIS   I'm cold. You know what I mean?   (Out front.)

KELLY

I'm hungry.   (Chews vigorously.)

MISS NADIA

Well, of course, you must be.   (She puts her arms around them.)   I was told by the courier that we would be met by a coachdriver called Master Landau.   (She reads the name from a piece of paper.)

MUSIC CUE 7

(They are startled by a cackle that emerges from the mist L. It is LANDAU, a toothless, misshapen creature, unkempt and unwashed, his left eye twitches incessantly.)

LANDAU

I have been sent to help you, Madam, and the - (Rubs hands.)   children. May I introduce myself?

MISS NADIA

Oh, please. Please do. Master Landau?

LANDAU

Master Landau indeed, Madam. Conceived in this dark place in sweltering lust, rejected by my father, and a victim of vengeance and hatred created by my mother. It is I who will lead you through the mists in this waiting carriage.

(He points to a number of painted tea-chests or stage blocks brought in by a number of Transylvanian VILLAGE IDIOTS. They make peculiar, unearthly noises and grunts as they go about the business of setting the coach. They touch the CHILDREN and find MISS NADIA a fascinating figure.)

Come. Quickly. The night draws in fast and it is not wise to be on the road late. Put those bags aloft, you scum.

(The IDIOTS pile the bags on and disappear.)

Come, my lady and - children. Please climb up on the carriage. We must be AWAY!

(There is a clap of thunder and the coach lurches forward to intro music of song. The CHILDREN and NADIA mime the action of pelting down steep ill-made roads on the swaying coach. The coach is simply stage blocks. They sit facing out front,

LANDAU high with a whip.)

MISS NADIA   Master Landau! You frighten me with your
urgency.

LANDAU   Urgency is the word, Madam. This is no place
for creatures of flesh and blood. You have come
to Transylvania. The edge of the world! Hiya!

(He cracks a whip and there is a neigh and another
clap of thunder, and the sound of hooves and
carriage wheels on stone.)

<u>MUSIC CUE 8</u>   (Optional number)

<u>SONG</u>: BE SILENT AND ATTENTIVE

LANDAU   Be silent and attentive to me
Hold fast as we pass the gallows tree
A dreadful creature devastates this land
Possessing woman and devouring man.

So we must ride, ride, ride
With never a backward glance.
Keep low and hide, hide, hide.
The inn is our only chance.

If the moon shines fair and bright
He will spy us from his castle height
When blood lust vampire dominates the air
Then 'fair is foul' and truly 'foul is fair'.

MISS NADIA,   So we must ride, ride, ride,
LANDAU &   With never a backward glance
PUPILS   Keep low and hide, hide, hide.
The inn is our only chance.

If the moon shines fair and bright
He will spy us from his castle height
When blood lust vampire dominates the air
Then 'fair is foul' and truly 'foul is fair'.

So we must ride, ride, ride,
With never a backward glance
Keep low and hide, hide, hide.
THE INN IS OUR ONLY CHANCE
IS OUR ONLY CHANCE!

LANDAU   Look, my lady. The inn, ahead.

MISS NADIA   Heaven be praised.

                  (They clamber down and move L. as LANDAU
                  signals IDIOTS to strike blocks and he and they
                  move, frightened shapes, to the wing R.)

                  Children, we've arrived safely here. And yet I
                  feel a sense of evil in this place. Can these be
                  people who shun God's good sunlight and go about
                  their lives behind drawn curtains? There is not a
                  soul to be seen.

LANDAU   That's as it may be, Ma'am. For myself, this is
                  as far as I go. You will find a warm fire and good
                  food at the inn of Master Hans and Frau Gretel. I
                  will say goodbye to you and the - children - and
                  wish you peace of mind in this dreadful place.

                  (Clap of thunder and he disappears into the mists.)

KELLY   Miss Naive. I think there are people here. I feel
                  as if a thousand eyes were watching us.

                  (Light comes up slowly behind gauze to reveal
                  GLUBLICK ADDICTS.)

ELVIS   Creepy. Know what I mean?   (Out front.)

                  (Faces start to appear in every possible nook and
                  cranny. They are lit by candles held in front of
                  their faces.)

                  MUSIC CUE 9

JULIE   Oh, Heavens, Miss Naive! Look! Look! Fiendish
                  manifestations! The spawn of Hell!

MISS NADIA   Don't be silly, Julie. You've been reading too many
                  books again!

JULIE   No, Miss. It is true. I see faces in the miasmic
                  mist.

MISS NADIA   Julie, you are right. But do not be afraid.

                  (The GLUBLICK ADDICTS start to move, slide,
                  breathe and grunt. They are misty figures appear-
                  ing behind the gauze - emerging from the grave-
                  yard.)

                  These bizarre faces may not be so mysterious.

(To audience.)   My strong belief in the basic
goodness which exists in all men may dispel your
doubts and fears.   Stop, creatures, and reveal
your identities.   (With large gesture.)

(She sweeps the PUPILS behind her like a hen with
her chicks.   The ADDICTS blow out their
individual candles as they call out their respective
names and on each name the main F.O.H. s
increase in intensity.)

IDIOTS

Clod –   Looby –   Scrub –   Scratch –
Riff –   Raff –   Bogie –   Boots –   Dregs –
Booze –   (He has great difficulty in blowing out
a flame.   The others all blow it out to his and
their delight.)

(The lights are fully up to reveal the inn and the
ADDICTS.   They all laugh and point to huge sign
descending: 'HANS UNT GRETEL BRAUHAUS'.)

KELLY

Why, they are simply the villagers.

JULIE

They are not the repugnant images that emanate
from my subconscious.

ELVIS

Still creepy though.   Know what I mean?   (Out
front.)

(The confrontation is broken by the entrance of
HERR HANS and FRAU GRETEL.   They are round
and jolly.)

HANS

Miss Nadia unt littel children velcome to our
humble inn.   All ze vay from Amerinka you are
coming.   Vat excitement.   Vat un adventure.

GRETEL

Indeed, velcome to the 'Brauhaus' of Herr Hans

(Signifies her husband, who bows.)

and Frau Gretel.   (She points to her husband
again.)

HANS

(whispering)   No, my little pumpkin – that is
you.

GRETEL

(sotto voce)   Me?

HANS

(sotto voce)   You-are-Frau-Gretel.

GRETEL	(loudly) Of course - me.
	(They all laugh.)
	I'm in such a whirl with the excitement.
MISS NADIA	Well, thank you for introducing yourselves and these must be the villagers?
KELLY	Strange attire.
JULIE	Spooky faces.
ELVIS	Weirdos - I like it.
MISS NADIA	They don't look at all well, Herr Hans.
	(There is a murmur of consternation from among the OUTPATIENTS.)
HANS	No, my dear, zere is no illness here.
	(The OUTPATIENTS shake their heads. No! No!)
GRETEL	Zere are no problems here.
	(The OUTPATIENTS more vigorously shake their heads. NO! NO!)
HANS	Well, maybe just a littel problem, but nuzzink to worry about. Nuzzink at all.
	(The OUTPATIENTS even more vigorously shake their heads with HANS and GRETEL. The whole stage is filled with shaking heads and 'No', 'No problems', etc.)
MISS NADIA	Herr Hans, the children and I are convinced that we are in safe hands - and we think your friends are absolutely cute.
JULIE	(removing glasses) Acceptable.
KELLY	Swell.
ELVIS	Right on.
GRETEL	Jah! Unt how excited they all haf been. Miss Nadia, we have been scrubbing ze bedrooms unt cooking ze food - so much activity zere has been.
HANS	Unt our friends have helped us mit every littel task. Is zat not true?

(The OUTPATIENTS intimate 'yes' with heads and jump up and down with anticipation.)

GRETEL   Ve cannot contain our euthanasia.

HANS   (correcting her quickly)   Enthusiasm.

GRETEL   (big, silly grin)   Oh, jah! Enthusiasm.

HANS   Unt delight. My dear teacher unt littel friends, truly, it is nize to 'ave you 'ere.

GRETEL   JAH! To 'ave you 'ere iz nize!

MUSIC CUE 10

SONG: NIZE TO 'AVE YOU 'ERE

(The OUTPATIENTS should be split into two distinct movement or dance groups. They move to the verses but have a strict comic routine for the chorus. Each group should be either side of the central playing area, which is occupied by HANS and GRETEL either side of NADIA and the CHILDREN. The principals' dance should be in direct contrast to the OUTPATIENTS'.)

HANS   We've been in a whirl
              Such a whirl unt a twirl
              We've been watchink for you noon unt night.
              Vot a scratchink of nails
              Vot a biting of heads
              We've been turning all our bedrooms inside-up.

CHORUS   But now you're here
              You betcha here
              Unt we mean it most sincere
              It's nize to 'ave you 'ere
              To 'ave you 'ere - it'z nize!

GRETEL   We've had such a bake
              Such a bake unt a boil
              We've been cookink for you noon unt night.
              Vot a bubblink of mash
              Vot a sausage of squeak
              We've been snitching all the schnitzels we could
                                                        snatch.

CHORUS   Good!
              But now you're here

You betcha here
And we mean it most sincere
It'z nize to 'ave you 'ere
To 'ave you 'ere - it'z nize.

NADIA &
PUPILS

(very American)
We've had such a trip
Such a wonderful flip
We've been travelling to you noon and night.
What a packing of planes
What a changing of bags
We've been looping all the loops that you could loop.

CHORUS

Fine!
But now we're (you're) here
You bet we're (cha) here
And we mean it most sincere.
It'z nize to be right ('ave you) 'ere
To be right (to 'ave you) 'ere iz nize!

ELVIS

Yea - but like - where is here? You know what I mean?

HANS

(aghast)   Vere is 'ere?   (He turns to
OUTPATIENTS and conducts them to speak.)

OUTPATIENTS

Vere is 'ERE?

HANS

Ve vill tell you vere is 'ere.   (Addressing
OUTPATIENTS.)   Gentlemen!

(They all straighten up as one.)

A small entertainment is required - we must sing
for our guests ze old song zat our fathers

(The OUTPATIENTS nod their heads syllabically
in time with the word 'father' from now on.)

unt our father's father, unt our -

OUTPATIENTS

(together)   - our father's father's father!

HANS

- taught us so long ago about the beauties of this our
beloved home town - Karloffia!

OUTPATIENTS

Karloffia! Karloffia! Karloffia! Karloffia!
Karloffia!

(The OUTPATIENTS sing the name of their beloved

town, a single voice followed by four separate units
moving as they sing to form a very tight, very
assymmetrical, very funny group R. Once they
arrive they should lean at forty-five degrees to the
right. They clip on plastic black moustaches as
they cross and hold onto the last 'Karloffia' until
BOOZE steps forward as conductor and signals
them to stop. The song is to be sung in the style
of a German barbers-shop quartet.
The song is conducted by BOOZE with much
feeling plus histrionics and he is at liberty to
either slow down or speed up the tune, or make it
lyrical or staccato as he thinks fit. He can even
extend the group into holding a note for too long.
In other words, he should play around and abuse
his power as conductor, though the 'choir' must be
totally Keaton-faced throughout.)

MUSIC CUE 11

SONG: KARLOFFIA

CHORUS   Karloffia
                 O sweet Karloffia
                 You are the lovelight in our eyes
                 Mit your orchards green
                 Unt your fields serene
                 We measure wisdom by the peace you bring,
                 The peace you bring.

                 Karloffia
                 O sweet Karloffia
                 You are the beacon in our night
                 Mit your steady beam
                 You light our darkest dreams
                 And keep us safely in the peace you bring,
                 The peace you bring.

                 (Sotto voce but the top line is sung as before and a
                 small group sing/talk the response.)

                 Karloffia
                     (Sunshine haven blessed by golden beams)
                 O sweet Karloffia
                     (Where the blossoms form a shady screen)
                 You are the lovelight in our eyes

(Dreaming all our simple secret dreams)
Mit your orchards green
    (See the petals floating down the sky)
Unt your fields serene
    (Azure letters whispering this reply)
We measure wisdom by the peace you bring
The peace you bring.

CHORUS

But now you're here
You betcha here
Unt we mean it most sincere
It'z nize to 'ave you 'ere
To 'ave you 'ere
In slightly pudderley, fairly mudderley, really
    cudderley, always luverly,
Karloffia
IT'Z NIZE!

HANS

So! You will like our Karloffia. Jah!

PUPILS

JAH!

GRETEL

Velcome littel ones. Come, you must be cold,
tired unt hungry after your long journey. Come.
Come inside by ze fire quickly.

(They enter the inn as HANS turns to the
OUTPATIENTS who are still smiling in a gleeful
freeze after the success of their song.)

HANS

Vell, don't just stand zere. You dummkopfs.
Zere is verk to be done. The bagg-age unt ze
lugg-age. It has to be unloaded. Come along.
You are like so much over-cooked sauer-kraut.
Tchaw!

<u>MUSIC CUE 12</u>

(They busily take the CHILDREN's bags, roll out
carpets to the entrance, set up tables, set props,
get chairs in place for the guests. This done
with much excitement, rustic expertise and
hospitality.)

MISS NADIA

This is truly wonderful, Herr Hans and Frau
Gretel. Bless you for your kindness and generosity.

HANS	It is nuzzink. Nuzzink. Quickly. Bring food.
	(Bread, cheese and ham appear on platters and they tuck in.)
GRETEL	Now, will that be enough food for you, my children?
JULIE	Truly overwhelming, Frau Gretel.
KELLY	Scrummy.
ELVIS	(his mouth is already full of bread but he makes a noise internally like:) This is great. You know what I mean?
GRETEL	Zat is fine. Fine. Now, while you eat and make yourselves comfortable, I will go unt prepare your rooms unt beds for tonight. Tonight in Karloffia you must sleep vell.

MUSIC CUE 13

(There is spooky incidental music and all freeze in position - HANS and GRETEL nose to nose.)

HANS	As vell as one may sleep who dvells below the shadow of the Castle of the Black Lake.
GRETEL	Hans, enough of such talk. You vill give the children nightmares. Do not listen to his stupid prattle. It is all nonsense.
HANS	Nonsense is it? Ask brother Clod if it was nonsense when they found his sister beneath those dark waters with the innumerable secrets of death and horror written on her tortured . face!
IDIOTS	Aye - Cloddy knows - horrible it was - true Herr Hans - etc. (They make agreements like mutineers encouraged by Long John Silver.)
HANS	But Gretel you are right, as alvays. Such talk may upset the children. Please. Please. Forgive me - an old man rambling.
JULIE	No, I'm interested.
	(They are agog, mouths open, food frozen in space.)
KELLY	Me, too.
ELVIS	I like creepy stuff - you know what I mean?

MISS NADIA	I think we have had enough of local legends and old folk tales for one evening. I think we should find those beds of ours and catch up on a little beauty sleep.
HANS	Sleep, she says!
	(HANS and GRETEL do a quick piece of Tyrolean hand slapping before repeating the word.)
	Sleep!
	(The IDIOTS all echo his amusement by repeating the word 'sleep'.)
	In Karloffia nobody goes to sleep unless zey 'ave drunk the famous local brew.
KELLY	Local brew?
GRETEL	Of course. It has marvellous qualities. Some say you can dream vatever you vish for.
ELVIS	Er - like what do you call this stuff, man?
HANS	We call it Glublick.
IDIOTS	(shout) GLUBLICK!
GRETEL	Indeed, it is called the Lubbly Glublick. I vonder if we have any around. (Winks.)
IDIOTS	Hi! (They all produce a hidden bottle from somewhere and plonk it on the table in a fifth of a second. The bottles can be attached to clips under the table.)
HANS	Gretel, the glasses quickly. Vould you like to hear about the lubbly Glublick, zat is made from our pure mountain vater and the secret herbs zat grow in ze valleys?
MISS NADIA	Why, Herr Hans, the children have done a little botany this year and this seems a splendid opportunity for some practical fieldwork. Please continue. It sounds most fascinating and deforming.
JULIE	Informing!
MISS NADIA	Informing - of course.
PUPILS	Sure. That's right. Tell us, please. What is

this Glublick stuff?

HANS   Very vell. But first charge your glasses and sing
viz me a chorus of the Lubbly Glublick Song. The
Lubbly Glublick!

MUSIC CUE 14

(They all raise their glasses and there are a great
range of fizzing, popping, glugging and plug pulling
noises. Then suddenly a smack of the lips followed
by a long sigh of 'aaaaaaaahhh'. They have glazed,
peaceful expressions.)

SONG: THE LUBBLY GLUBLICK SONG

HANS   (on a chair)
If you're a poor man who is full of regret
From family matters and problems of debt
If you've done all you can, but would like to do more,
Then drink up your Glublick and freedom's restored.

CHORUS   Drink Lubbly Glublick
Fill up your glass to the brim
Drink Lubbly Glublick
Till it o'erflows the rim.
All your troubles will stop
You'll find peace in each drop
When Glublick goes FIZZ   (Make the noise.)
PING   (Hit glass with something.)
and POP!   (Finger in cheek. Or leave it all to
percussion section and hooters.)

GRETEL   (on a table)
If you're a housewife who has given her all
To Wiener Schnitzel and Pumpernick balls.
If you've done all you can, and the meal has no spice
Then pop in some Glublick, and everyzink's nice!

CHORUS   Drink Lubbly Glublick
Fill up your glass to the brim.
Drink Lubbly Glublick
Till it o'erflows the rim.
All your troubles will stop
You'll find peace in each drop
When Glublick goes FIZZ, PING and POP!

(Enter WELLY BOOT DANCERS onto catwalks and

central well.)

IDIOTS

(each character blurts out his name and waves as
he sings it in the song)
If you're a LOOBY, a CLOD or RIFF-RAFF,
You'll like drinking Glublick with SCRUB and with
    SCRATCH.
If you've drunk all you can, and there's DREGS in
    your BOOTS
Then pass on the Glublick to BOGIE and BOOZE!

(Each character sings his own name, a quick way
of reminding the audience who they are - plus a
chance for rustic idiocy 'business'.
The WELLY BOOT DANCERS should dance an
Austrian hand and boot slapping dance - in pairs or
groups. Noisy and funny.)

CHORUS

Drink Lubbly Glublick
Fill up your glass to the brim
Drink Lubbly Glublick
Till it o'erflows the rim
All your troubles will stop
You'll find peace in each drop
When Glublick goes FIZZ, PING and POP!

PUPILS

If you're a schoolchild who finds learning too tough
And equations confuse you, then never give up
If you've done all you can, still the figures perplex
Just dip them in Glublick, the answer is 'x'.

ALL

Drink Lubbly Glublick
Fill up your glass to the brim
Drink Lubbly Glublick
Till it o'erflows the rim.
All your troubles will stop
When Glublick goes FIZZ, PING and POP!

HURRAH!

HANS

Excellent. Excellent. But ze evening draws in,
my friends, and much as ve love Karloffia in ze
day, zere are many zings we fear in ze night.

GRETEL

Yes, Hans, it is time zat ze inn vas closed for ze
night. Ze darkness is thickening

(Wind sound effect.)

and a vind springing up. So, my village customers,
when I clap my hands - like ze Karloffia rats,
(She winks at this harmless piece of imagery.)
you must return to your holes.

MUSIC CUE 15

(GRETEL claps her hands and they strike two side
tables, leaving the table C. All this should be done
in five seconds, even though they appear to get in
each other's way.)

HANS	Soon zey vill be safely home unt in zere beds.
GRETEL	And talking of beds, come, children, it is late and I expect you have a busy day tomorrow.
MISS NADIA	Yes. That is true. Quickly, children - down the stairs and off to bed.
GRETEL	Come. I vill show you the vay. (She takes a lantern from the table and guides them to one large simple trestle bed on the catwalk R. It has a large patchwork quilt.)
JULIE	Goodnight all, and thanks for the Glublick.
KELLY	See you at breakfast.
ELVIS	Like - er - bye-byes - you know what I mean?
	(GRETEL takes them to the bed and they snuggle in without undressing. They pop on colourful nightcaps.)
GRETEL	Sleep tight, little ones.
MISS NADIA	(speaks as she returns) Your talk of evils imminent may have disturbed the children a little - but I am not nervous. I believe that in some uncharted forgotten corner of the world there is a force of good that will stand defiant against the teeth of evil and the jaws of death!
GRETEL	Little Nadia - zis is amazink. You haf described to ze very life a close friend of ours. A young handsome man -
MISS NADIA	Oh -
GRETEL	Jah - a young handsome man - dedicated, bold unt fearless!

HANS — Jah, zat is so. Dr Nick Necrophiliac is his name, a brilliant young English man of medicine. He has been residink with us here at the 'Brauhaus' while he continues his scientific studies at nearby Heidelberg University.

MISS NADIA — Why he sounds tremonstrous. A dream man and English, too! My own long lost ancestors came from that green and pleasant land.

GRETEL — Iz this true vat you are sayink?

MISS NADIA — Indeedy-so. They were born in the great city of Birmingcrumb. But where does this doctor you talk of come from?

HANS — Nobody knows - exactly. But we do know that he is valiunt and couraijus. How do you say in ze English legends, a brave Sir Gollyhead (Galahad).

GRETEL — Indeed, a positive action-man.

(There is a knock at the door rhythmically rapped to the first line of 'Rule Britannia' which is highlighted by the tune on a piano with one finger.)

Why, there is his familiar knock and he will be accompanied by his close friend, Father O'Stake (She forgets her domestic duties and speaks all this in one breath.) who sailed across the narrow seas from the mists of Ireland to be the doctor's constant companion and advisor in their fight against the black arts.

HANS — Gretel?

GRETEL — Hans?

HANS — Isn't zat ze door zat I am hearink? Please open ze up. Our friends will be cold unt tired.

GRETEL — Of course. Vat am I sinkin' of?

(Looks out front or collects NICK and FATHER O'STAKE from the wings.)

It is as ve unticipated. Come in. Father O'Stake.

(They clasp each other, then he moves across to shake hands with HANS.)

HANS	Doctor. Father. It is good to see your honest and kind faces in zese parts again.
GRETEL	Indeed it is and ve have a surprise for you, my friends. See a pretty young teacher has come from Amerinka with her pupils.
NICK	I am charmed to meet you, Madam.
	(He kisses NADIA's hand. She is flustered.)
O'STAKE	God bless you, my child, and keep you in his safe hands.
MISS NADIA	Well, I'm sure I'm very pleased to meet you both, gentlemen.
	(The whole COMPANY freeze in a shaped group. Two tight separate spots come up on the faces of NADIA and NICK as they speak. It is done like the worst soundtrack of the worst Hollywood romantic film ever to issue from MGM. They move towards each other in slow motion speed like a hair shampoo advertisement. They move throughout the dialogue in this way.)

MUSIC CUE 16

NICK	Like steel and a magnet we have been drawn together here in this town. I feel it in my very soul.
	(Pretty SINGERS float in to catwalk L. in slow motion.)
MISS NADIA	There is a time for talk and a time for quiet. This is such a time. I must just look upon him. He is truly a man with whom a woman can feel safe. And I am sure he is well qualified.
NICK	I feel breathless in this strange and total silence. I will never forget this one night when destiny has brought us together if only for a short while. If only I could speak to her, tell her that I love her, that I worship her, that I am well qualified!
MISS NADIA	(out front after a quick breathless run to L.) This man has a dauntless front. I recognise in him all those qualities essential to the creation of a white crusader. He has my heart for this is

the first time I have ever been face to face with a positive (Deep inward breath.) action (Outward gasp.) man. (Flutters eyes.)

(GRETEL, HANS and FATHER O'STAKE move their right hands to heart on word 'positive', then left hand to forehead, palm out, on 'action', then slow lower of both hands on word 'man'.)

NICK

(running to R., out front) And you - must be - (Looks her over.) WOMAN!

(Explosive chord into song. NICK whirls round to C.)

MUSIC CUE 17

(NICK starts song at C. Pretty GIRLS on catwalk L. NADIA, HANS, GRETEL and FATHER O'STAKE form a group U.R. They move in a kind of 'Pans People' routine.)

SONG: POSITIVE ACTION MAN

NICK (together)	PRETTY GIRLS
Look at me walk	Look at him walk
Hear me talk	Hear him talk
A cool lovin'	A cool lovin'
Hammer Horror	Hammer Horror
Groovin-movin-man	Groovin-movin-man

I'm a positive action man.................!

NADIA, HANS, GRETEL, O'STAKE

(after each line above, together)
Super-cinematic
Warner Panchromatic
A cool lovin'
Hammer Horror
Groovin-movin-man
He's a positive action man!

NICK & GIRLS	NADIA et al
Positive action	Zip-Zap-Pow-Slap
Satisfaction	Biff-bang Crunch-crack!
'Universal' chivalry	'Universal' chivalry
Positive action	Zip-zap-pow-slap

Stimulaction
'Paramount' sublimity
Oh
Yea!
He's for me
Super 'X' certificate
Hercules
I'm a positive action man!

Biff-bang-crunch-crack
'Paramount' sublimity
Oh
(Yea) yea!
(He's for me) me!
Super 'X' certificate
Hercules
He's a positive action
                      man!

NICK

PRETTY GIRLS

Look at me move
Watch me groove
A cool lovin'
Hammer Horror
Groovin-movin-man
I'm a positive action man..................!

Look at him move
Watch him groove
A cool lovin'
Hammer Horror
Groovin-movin-man

NADIA, HANS, GRETEL, FATHER O'STAKE

(at the same time as above)
Ooo-boo-bee-doo-bee
Ooo-boo-bee-doo-bee
A cool lovin'
Hammer Horror
Groovin-movin-man
He's a positive action man.

NICK & GIRLS

NADIA et al

Positive action
Satisfaction
'Gaumont-British'
          ecstasy
Positive action
Kung Fu Fraction
'Warner Brothers'
          gallantry
Oh
Yea!
He's for me
Super three dimensional
Mystery
I'm a positive action man!

Zip-Zap-Pow-Slap
Biff-bang-crunch-crack!
'Gaumont-British'
          ecstasy
Zip-zap-pow-slap
Fried rice lips smack
'Warner Brothers'
          gallantry
Oh
(Yea) yea!
(He's for me) me!
Super three dimensional
Mystery
He's a positive action
                      man!

GIRLS et al	ELECTRIC MAN
NICK	(spoken) True to my word will I be-ee-ee-ee-ee
GIRLS et al	FROM SILVER SCREEN
NICK	True as steel, just wait and see-ee-ee-ee-ee
GIRLS et al } NICK }	DISINTEGRATE GODZILLA You will not need to thank me
GIRLS et al } NICK }	STOP THE QUATERMASS MACHINE I've done roamin' with Polanski
GIRLS et al	DOCTOR MAN
NICK	Fighting for Right, will I strive
GIRLS et al	FROM RKO
NICK	Samuel Goldwyn is my guide
GIRLS et al } NICK }	PLEASE SQUASH THE SPIDER WOMAN I will squash the Spider Woman
GIRLS et al } NICK }	NEUTRALISE THE GIANT CLAM Neutralise the Giant Clam

(During next lines OTHERS make a 'heavenly hum'.

NADIA

Please make him go
That E. A. Poe
'Cos whenever he's around
It's Usher, Usher, Usher
And we all fall down!

NICK	PRETTY GIRLS
Look at me walk	Look at him walk
Hear me talk	Hear him talk
A cool lovin'	A cool lovin'
Hammer Horror	Hammer Horror
Grovin-movin-man	Groovin-movin-man
I'm a positive action man...................!	

NADIA, HANS, GRETEL, FATHER O'STAKE

(at the same time as above)
Super-cinematic
Warner Panchromatic
A cool lovin'

Hammer Horror
Groovin-movin-man
He's a positive action man!

NICK & GIRLS	NADIA et al
Positive action	Zip-Zap-Pow-Slap
Satisfaction	Biff-bang-crunch-crack!
'Universal' chivalry	'Universal' chivalry
Positive action	Zip-zap-pow-slap
Stimulaction	Biff-bang-crunch-crack!
'Paramount' sublimity	'Paramount' sublimity
Oh	Oh
Yea!	(Yea) yea!
He's for me .	(He's for me) me!
Super 'X' certificate	Super 'X' certificate
Hercules	Hercules
I'm a positive action	I'm a positive action
Not a matter of faction	Not a matter of faction
But a	But a
POSITIVE	POSITIVE
ACTION	ACTION

NICK   (spoken out front)   Got the picture?

                MAN!   MAN!

HANS   And now, gentlemen,

                (His voice breaks the freeze and there is
                animation once again.)

                it is time zat you also vere fed and warmed.
                Gretel, food for Dr Nicholas and Father O'Stake.

O'STAKE   God bless you, Herr Hans. And Gretel, I see
                it's your home cooking we'll be having?

GRETEL   Indeed. Indeed.

                (They laugh and take places at the table.)

NICK   A magnificent spread, dear friends.

                (They tuck in.)

O'STAKE   Miss Nadia, you are here for a holiday?
                Sightseeing, perhaps?

MISS NADIA   That is so, Father. We hope to visit some of

your lovely towns and make a number of historical
excursions to your ancient castles.

(They stop eating immediately and exchange grave
and meaningful looks.)

NICK   I would venture no further than the lovely towns,
            Nadia. There are many superstitions appertaining
            to some of our castles and it is wise not to search
            too deeply into their origins.

HANS   Listen vell to his vords.

            (The wind strengthens and the lights dim subtly.)

GRETEL   There are things here of vhich ze children should
            have no knowledge. Believe us.

MISS NADIA But surely it would be foolish not to extend our
            knowledge of European History while resident in
            Transylvania.

            (During DR NICK's tale we see CLOD behind the
            gauze re-enact the scene in mime.)

            MUSIC CUE 18

NICK   Nadia, shall I tell you about the most recent piece
            of history in our country?

            (She nods. He looks at the others and after a pause
            they nod their assent.)

            Last year an old and revered man of our village
            died. It is customary here to dig the graves in
            rows. As Clod, our gravedigger, was making a
            new grave he heard sounds of knocking proceeding
            from the very grave in which his sister had been
            buried but a few days previously. Terrified, he
            came to see me, knowing of my recent research into
            life beyond death

            (He hands her a card. She reacts: Ooo!)

            and together we called on Father O'Stake who
            granted permission for the grave to be opened.
            When we returned the cries still issued from the
            tomb, when we opened the coffin we discovered the
            body of the woman still warm, her arms and face
            scratched and bleeding. But here is the moment

when we realised the awful truth of the matter.
On her neck we saw the unmistakable marks of the
vampire. She was possessed.

(They all scream a short, sharp, staccato scream.)

GRETEL

I still shudder at this tale.

O'STAKE

Peace. Peace. Frau Gretel, do not upset
yourself. It was a year ago now and the Lord be
praised we have had no more of it.

HANS

Many vhispered in the village that Count Dracula
had returned to his castle and that he and his evil
mother had come vonce again to feed on ze people
of our village.

GRETEL

Ve should have no fear of him now – he has been
dead some fifty years and ze Castle of the Black
Lake stands empty.

MUSIC CUE 19

O'STAKE

Dead? Or merely sleeping?

NICK

Well observed, Father, for the vampire may regain
its powers if it can but obtain the life-force blood
it craves from one who is sufficiently pure and
innocent.

(After the word 'innocent', they all look at NADIA
very quickly together and then away. This should
be done very, very quickly.)

MISS NADIA

I may appear to you very naive – but what exactly
is a vampire?

NICK

Father O'Stake? (He intimates that such an
explanation is best given by a man of God.)

O'STAKE

(talking as if giving a supernatural sermon)
The vampire, my child, is the re-animated body
of a dead person, believed to come from the grave
and wander by night, sucking the blood of persons
asleep or hypnotised, causing their death.

NICK

The vampire can sense the spilt blood of an innocent
over thousands of miles and in the form of a bat
will fly in search of his victim.

MISS NADIA   But is there no protection against such an evil
                 creature of the dark?

HANS   The vampire fears both garlic and running water.

GRETEL   Glass and holy oil.

O'STAKE   The cross of our Lord.

NICK   And the sharpened wooden stake which brings
                 everlasting death.

MISS NADIA   It's horrible. Horrible.

                 <u>MUSIC CUE 20</u>

                 (Suddenly the lights dim, there is a distant
                 rumble of thunder and the sound of a coach being
                 driven wildly and pulling up outside the inn. All
                 are frozen in horror.)

                 What is it?

NICK   Have no fear, Nadia. Stand firm everyone.

O'STAKE   This is a late night visitor none of us wish to
                 welcome.

NICK   Hans, quickly – the garlic!

                 (HANS hands out sprigs of protective garlic,
                 abhorred by the vampire.)

NADIA   Please, won't someone tell me what this is all
                 about?

O!STAKE   You are about to meet the fount of evil on earth,
                 my child.

                 (She starts.)

                 Yes, I know it is difficult to conceive of evil made
                 flesh, but Count Dracula is such a creature.

                 <u>MUSIC CUE 21(A)</u>

                 (The door bursts open, there is a crash of thunder
                 and lightning lights the face of COUNT DRACULA.
                 A wind blows behind him and leaves are blown
                 across the stage from the open door. He is wet.
                 All shrink back except NICK who stands firm.)

NICK   What draws your evil presence to this simple inn?

Your blackness best befits only the darkness of your accursed castle.

DRACULA   (speaking slowly and smoothly)   My dear young doctor, how rude and abrupt is your welcome. (He removes white gloves slowly.)

GRETEL   (bravely)   Not as rude and abrupt as your exit shall be, dear Count, if your purpose is to feed on the souls and bodies of the simple people of this town.

DRACULA   Take care, my dear lady, tonight you have the safety and protection of your inn.   Another day – who knows?

GRETEL   We are not afraid of you.

DRACULA   NO!   I can hazard a guess that these simpletons (Points to the others.)   are only 'here for the fear'.

O'STAKE   Fearful we may be, Count Dracula, but our belief in the Church and all that it stands for is protection enough from your powers.

DRACULA   Come, my friends, do you not know that my visionary eyes can pierce even the deepest gloom of the darkest grave? And my eyes have such a vision now, but this time of beauty and light. A jewel of rare quality. Mademoiselle, I see that you are a woman of some culture, you must forgive the coarseness of this riff-raff, these stories of an evil reputation are but figments of their imaginations.

                 (He goes to NADIA, takes her hand and kisses it.)

MISS NADIA   (swept off her tiny feet)   You are most 'charmant', Count.

NICK   Beware, Nadia, do not be fooled by his fair words and flattery.

DRACULA   The doctor, my dear, has never been a great admirer of me or my life's work – which is strange for we are both in our way experts in simple surgery. It must be something of a 'dying art', eh, Doctor?

NICK   Inhuman phantom! Why are you here? Be about
                your business and leave. Or you shall deal with me.

MISS NADIA   (impressed)   Oh!

DRACULA   Really. Such insults. They put my teeth on edge.
                (Aside to audience.)   If I could but possess some
                small part of this girl's belongings – some small
                trinket so I could have power over her. Then I
                could sup some of the life blood I crave –
                (Insanely.)   blood which is wasted in her pretty
                mindless body.   (To NADIA, coolly.)   My
                dear, my business is but a simple proposition. I
                am a man of immense wealth and would be willing
                to pay you handsomely if you would be so kind as to
                call at my ancestral home. I have a number of –
                er – daughters who are much in need of private
                tuition. I would be your undying master – er –
                servant, if you would agree to give them some
                short lessons in, say, etiquette and deportment.
                I assure you, they would be very willing pupils
                and hang on your every word.   (He stretches out
                a hand to her face.)   I feel with your experience
                you could excite their interest and stir their blood!
                (He deftly removes one of NADIA's earrings.)

MISS NADIA   Oh. You are most kind, sir. We shall need some
                extra money for our vacation. Yes, I shall be glad
                to accept your kind invitation.

OTHERS   No, Nadia. Nadia, do not go. etc. This is
                foolish. Think, girl.

DRACULA   (interrupting their protests)   Splendid. I shall
                expect you tomorrow night for dinner then. I
                always have an exceptional appetite in the
                evenings!

                (He smiles to reveal his fangs. NADIA is caught
                in his hypnotic stare. As he moves towards her
                the OTHERS produce the garlic and he cringes
                back.)

                Forgive me, my dear, a sudden illness, an old
                allergy with which I suffer from time to time. I
                shall look forward to our first lessons tomorrow
                night. Farewell.

MUSIC CUE 21 (B)

(DRACULA exits through the door, there is a
crash of thunder and wind howls. The coach is
heard clattering away. HANS runs to the door and
watches him depart - but NADIA is still in a trance.)

HANS

All is well. He has gone. Only the night mist
remains.

O'STAKE

(noticing that NADIA is still in a trance)   NADIA!

(He flicks his fingers in front of her face and she
awakens.)

Wake from this trance!

MISS NADIA

My goodness me. I'm sorry. I must have been
dreaming.

O'STAKE

You must not dream, child, nor gaze at me in
vacant stare. Your dream was real enough and I
strongly advise you not to venture into the castle of
Count Dracula.

NICK

Listen well, Nadia, for Father O'Stake speaks wise
words.

MISS NADIA

Of course. You are right. I shall not go. But it
seemed for a moment as if he had some power over
my thoughts! No, I shall not go. Tomorrow it
will be sightseeing first and then we must travel on.

HANS

Good girl.

GRETEL

Sensible. Very sensible.

O'STAKE

And now I must travel on.

(They laugh and NICK prepares to join him.)

No, Dr Nick, it would be better if you stayed here
the night and persuaded our young teacher to forget
about her promise to start evening classes.
Goodnight and God protect you in His infinite wisdom.

(They say farewells at the door and HANS turns to
yawn.)

GRETEL

Goodnight, good Father.

HANS

Come, Gretel, we too must sleep. The night draws

	in and we have a long day ahead of us tomorrow.
GRETEL	Yes, yes. You are right, Hans. Here I have the bottles ready.
	(She produces - or picks up from food tray - two enormous hot water bottles marked 'HANS' and 'HERS'. They slip on brightly coloured nightcaps and exit, saying:)
HANS } GRETEL }	Goodnight, young friends.
NICK	Goodnight both.
MISS NADIA	And sleep well.
HANS } GRETEL }	(their voices fading) Ve vill. Ve vill.
	(NADIA and NICK are alone and take this opportunity to discuss the events but they are still a little shy.)
MISS NADIA	Doctor, I found tonight's events conflictin' and confusin'.
NICK	It is confusin' - er - fusing, Nadia. You see, there exist certain beings whose very lives seem bound by invisible chains to the supernatural - Count Dracula is such a one. He seeks therefore the solitude of his castle. He dwells there all alone, save for his crazed mother, the Countess Wraith, and his faithful servant, Genghis.
MISS NADIA	You seem to know an awful lot about him.
NICK	I do. My studies have convinced me that this man is truly what we have come to recognise as a vampire. And my researches at Heidelberg University prove that vampirism is not physical but supernatural. (He hands her a card.) There is, of course, only one cure for such an occult disease.
MISS NADIA	A cure? What, in Heaven's name?
NICK	It is too terrible to relate to such innocent ears. Come, enough of this talk. You must rest. Give me your hand.
	(NICK takes her hand. There are immediately the

voices of a hidden heavenly choir humming 'Just
the Way' as he leads NADIA to the catwalk L.)

MISS NADIA   You are very gallant. Kind and gentle. Well –
                  hush my mouth – here I am talking away to you and
                  I don't even know your first name.

NICK   I hardly like to say – my name is Nicholas Orlando
                  Erasmus Cecil Necrophiliac. I know –   (Puts
                  up his hand to prevent her speaking.)   it is a
                  stupid and ridiculous name.

MISS NADIA   It is not at all. Heavens, what's in a name? It's
                  just a string of words. I like you for what you
                  are, Nicholas, not your name. Goodnight now.

NICK   Goodnight.

                  MUSIC CUE 22

                  (NADIA descends to the catwalk R. while NICK
                  goes to catwalk L. There is a chair set on each
                  area. NADIA slips off her jacket and starts to
                  comb her hair in preparation for bed. A spot
                  comes up on each area and the children asleep.
                  NICK looks up from his chair and sings. He is
                  reading a bedtime book.)

                  SONG: JUST THE WAY

NICK   What's in a name, she says
                  It's just a string of words.
                  She takes me at face value
                  She likes me as I am.

                  So let me stay
                  Just the way
                  Just the way she likes me.
                  For the way she likes me
                  Is just the way I am.

                  No need for complications
                  Romantic affectations
                  She's the kind of someone
                  Who likes me
                  Just the way I am.

So let me stay
Just the way
Just the way she likes me.
For the way she likes me
Is just the way I am.

MISS NADIA   Someone to hold me, someone to bless
Someone to sweep up for, when there's a mess.
Someone to stir up, if it's only a part
Of the fire that warms the chill of my heart.
Someone to need me, someone to share
Someone to love me, hold me, take me, need me,
  want me, care for me.

So let me stay
Just the way
Just the way he likes me
For the way he likes me
Is just the way I am.
(Repeat together.)

(The song may be repeated with backing group.)

NICK   (looking across at NADIA) Goodnight, Nadia,
and - sweet dreams. (Blows out his spot light.)

MISS NADIA   (solus) Goodnight, doctor - with the funny name.
(Blows out spot light.)

(They and CHILDREN exit in darkness.)

HOUSE LIGHTS UP

ACT TWO

MUSIC CUE 23

House lights down. Empty stage or area except
for unlit figures of NADIA, DRACULA and GENGHIS.
COMPANY sing in the wings (sotto voce).

SONG: THE DRACULA SPECTACULA SHOW!

(Reprise)

LOOK! READ! GASP! QUIVER!
He's waiting for you there
GIRL!

(Spot picks up NADIA's face C. She is in a pose
like a comic strip beauty.)

MEETS!
GHOUL!

(Spot picks up DRACULA and GENGHIS close
together drooling over her body.)

SHIVER!

(Black light ballet:

Dance group of ZOMBIE MEN/BRIDES OF
DRACULA enter and move to following as NADIA
spins off. Rest of COMPANY sing in the wings.
The ZOMBIE MEN dressed in black hooded drapes,
white faces, and black rimmed circular eyes.
BRIDES in white hooded drapes and white paper
'Afro' wigs. The DANCERS lit by black light (U.V.)
To get maximum effect paint all white accessories
in any washing powder solution or wash garments
in concentrated washing powder solution. No other
lights should be on except ultra violet.)

So if you feel cosy
With Bela Lugosi
This is the show for you.
There are no tomorrows
In this chamber of horrors
Check your heart-rate - do.

Who is it drinks from the coffin's cup?

What goes down, but must come up?
The Prince of Vampires, the King of Night.
It's the Dracula Spectacula
The Dracula Spectacula
The Dracula Spectacula Show!

BAT! SCREECH! BLOOD! RITES!
You'll need the exorcise.
WHITE! FANGS! EYES! ICE!
Do not trust that smile.

So if your cuppa tea
Could be Christopher Lee
Then fly with us tonight
'Cos it's a two-way trip
In a cataleptic fit
Watch out in case he bites!

Who is it drinks from the coffin's cup?
What goes down, but must come up?
The Prince of Vampires, the King of Night.
It's the Dracula Spectacula
The Dracula Spectacula
The Dracula Spectacula Show!

(Scream and exit on blackout.
Then area a sudden blaze of light as follow spots
pick up DRACULA (purple) and GENGHIS (blue) as
they burst in from R. and L. respectively. They
cackle in standard ghoul fashion, cross C. and go to
opposite sides of the stage and cackle a second time.
They turn and look at each other.)

DRACULA   One more, I think, Genghis?

GENGHIS   Indeed, Master.

(They cross and cackle for the third time. Although
they both obviously relish the chance to do it a third
time, DRACULA suddenly interrupts the cackle of
GENGHIS which is overplayed by belabouring and
striking GENGHIS.)

DRACULA   Crook-backed fool! Kneeling there, quivering,

(GENGHIS quivers.)

with the castle keys trembling in your deformed

hands.

(Keys rattle.   They have spiders dangling from them.)

I am impatient with your tardiness.

GENGHIS   Master, I have tried. If you only knew how hard I have tried. I have done my best in preparing the rooms and the lower chamber for your guests.

DRACULA   But you work so slowly, imbecile.

(GENGHIS hides behind DRACULA.)

Can you do nothing faster?   You know that tonight everything must be as we have planned.

GENGHIS   As we have planned.   (His head appears over DRACULA's left shoulder as he speaks and then disappears.)

DRACULA   After tonight, more of my creatures will walk abroad, and all will see and acknowledge my genius. I will be master of both the living and the dead!

GENGHIS   – the living and the dead.   (His head appears below DRACULA's right knee as he speaks.)

DRACULA   (observes him side-spied)   Careful fool! Remember I will choose carefully those of my servants who are worthy enough to be allowed the honour of serving me through eternity.

(He is frenetic and his palsied left arm starts to rise.   GENGHIS copies the movement and they smack the offending limbs into place together.)

GENGHIS   Let me be among them, master. I will assist you in all work. I will find fresh material to aid us. (He goes to exit and is stopped.)

DRACULA   Ectoplasmic cretin! Have I not found the victims already. Now go, dog, and prepare the life-blood substitute in the laboratory of the North Tower –

(Slowly turning to him – GENGHIS knows what is coming.)

or it will be –

<u>MUSIC CUE 24</u>

GENGHIS   No! No!

DRACULA   – the Black Lake and its murky depths for your
deformed trunk!

GENGHIS   (screams and then launches himself into the
biggest piece of overacting ever witnessed on the
British stage)   Not the Black Lake, Master!
I already feel its cold watery grip about my neck,
the clutching weeds and the drowned voices of your
countless victims screaming below the surface.
No, not the Black Lake. Mercy, I cry, mercy,
Master –

DRACULA   (quietly)   Genghis.

GENGHIS   (rushing to R., by now too caught up in the
performance)   Anything but a muddy grave at
the bottom of that dreaded Lake – please, Master,
please –

DRACULA   (louder)   Genghis!

GENGHIS   Not the Black Laaaaake –

DRACULA   GENGHIS!

GENGHIS   Master?   (Subdued.)

DRACULA   (pointing offstage)   The North Tower.

GENGHIS   The North Tower, Master.   (He exits L.,
halting at the pro arch, out front.)   Nobody
understands me!

(There is an unearthly subterranean noise below
stage, if possible. It is the COUNTESS WRAITH.)

DRACULA   Mother, is that you?

(More noises.)

Mother, we have some visitors this evening. I
think you should join us.

(He pulls a ratchet rope and opens the trap, smoke
pours out of it, it is green, and from it emerges the
figure of the COUNTESS WRAITH. She is dressed
in grey weeds and upon emerging cleans herself off,

showering the stage with dust.)

WRAITH   Dracula, my son, my boy, why do you keep your
            mother imprisoned below in the dungeons and
            vaults at the edge of the steaming lakes?

DRACULA   Because of your constant chatter, Mother, and –

            (COUNTESS WRAITH starts to hum a single,
            spooky note – arms outstretched.)

            MUSIC CUE 25   (Incidental music)

WRAITH   (going into a trance – she is a charlatan)
            And soothing thus the dreamer's pains
            My Dracula will drink the life blood from their
                veins.

DRACULA   – and your ridiculous chanting of verse from the
            past!

WRAITH   Not ridiculous, not ridiculous, Draccy.

DRACULA   (stamping his foot, 'camp')   Mother ! I forbid
            you to call me by that name.

WRAITH   But it is the name I remember you by, when as a
            child you first knelt by your mother's throat.
            Oh, Draccy – not ridiculous.   (She stops. She
            is serious and addresses the audience.)
            I have had a vision!

DRACULA   Not another sea of blood!   (Despairing.)

            MUSIC CUE 26   (Incidental music)

WRAITH   (in a phoney trance again, with hum)   I see – a
            sea of blood and out of it comes a figure dressed in
            white. He holds the jagged stake above his head
            and down, down it plunges. I see you, my son,
            falling from the black sky, writhing in a hell of
            agony as you fall, fall into the vast void of ever-
            lasting death.
            Now shall Dracula be destroyed by 'he',
            O living memorial to my agony.
            The man in white shall halt our task
            And banish both to tomb and dust!

            (Out of trance.)   There, I feel much better now.

(During this sequence we see NICK lit behind gauze. He re-enacts the scene described above in mist and slow motion. It is a dream effect.)

DRACULA   Silence, Mother, enough of this foolish rhyme. I see no obstacles in our pathway - do you?

WRAITH   No.

(They both cackle hysterically. COUNTESS WRAITH gets covered with dust, DRACULA exposes his fangs.)

DRACULA   Come, Mother-in-Blood. We have the Life Blood Experiment to complete in the North Tower. I shall call Genghis.

WRAITH   Yes, the substitute. I feel weaker already and my vision's become less clear.

DRACULA   Fool! Genghis! The North Tower!

GENGHIS   (offstage)   I am coming as fast as I can, Master.

DRACULA   Why does he test me so? Genghis, you should have come earlier.

GENGHIS   (entering)   Why? What did I miss?

DRACULA   Nothing, you fool. I mean you should have been here earlier with the Tower. Is it ready?

GENGHIS   Yes, Master. I have it outside.

DRACULA   Well, don't just stand there drooling, crookback dog! Bring it in!

(GENGHIS drags in a complete tower on wheels, built on a scaffolding tower complete with crackpot laboratory and smoke. It is clearly labelled 'The North Tower'. There should be enough room for DRACULA to stand on the platform.)

Excellent.

WRAITH   Fangtastic!

(They all cackle outrageously.)

DRACULA   If the experiment works then soon my creatures will walk abroad throughout the earth and all men will acknowledge my mastery over life and death!

Listen closely,   (To GENGHIS.)   deformed
slave, and   (To COUNTESS WRAITH.)
putrefied parent, once we have created a life blood
substitute we may have living death at our disposal.
You realise the significance of such power?

GENGHIS ⎫ WRAITH ⎭	(together, nodding heads) Yees –
DRACULA	(annoyed that they realise it) What!
GENGHIS ⎫ WRAITH ⎭	(together, shaking heads) No – Nooooo!
DRACULA	The significance is – everlasting evil – eternal world dominance. We shall become predators with supreme power! (They all cackle.)
WRAITH	I knew you would go far, Draccy. (DRACULA's look of contempt is interrupted by:)
GENGHIS	O, Master., I grovel and fawn at your feet. You are indeed master of all!
DRACULA	Of course, and shall I tell you why?
GENGHIS⎫ WRAITH ⎭	Tell us! TELL US!
DRACULA	Because I have the supreme gift.
GENGHIS⎫ WRAITH ⎭	The supreme gift?
DRACULA	GENIUS!
GENGHIS	(spelling it out) J – E – N –
WRAITH	Y – U – S.
ALL	GENIUS!
GENGHIS	But how do we lesser immortals acquire this gift, Master?
WRAITH	Give us the formula of this secret.
DRACULA	There is no formula, fools – (His sham Etonian accent suddenly crumbles in his excitement.) you either 'ave it or you do not

'ave it. I 'appen to 'ave it!

MUSIC CUE 27

A genius - one in a thousand. Because to be a
genius, my pathetic underlings, one must have not
only flair,

(A silver top hat is thrown in from the wing.)

style,   (He puts on hat.)   and sophistication -

(A silver cane is thrown in from the the wing.)

one must have an overpowering hatred for all others
who stand in your way.

SONG: A SUPER RAT LIKE ME

(spoken)
Don't let this tale of vanity
Appear as mere profanity

(sings, patter style)
Let me prepare you, if I may
For what I'm going to say.
Simply mould your education
On human exploitation
And, if you can stand the test,
You could be up here with the best
Listen to a connoisseur of crime -

(singing and dancing - the dance should be
extremely 'stagey' and in the 'hat and cane' style
of Frankie 'Showbiz' Vaughan)
If you want flair - style - sophistication
Smart - witty - conversation
In your struggle to the top
You must let the others rot
If you wanna be a super-rat like me
If you wanna be a super-rat like me.

(speaking)   Let me give you an example

(singing)
You plan a dinner, at two or three
A cosy 'auberge', beside the sea
This wealthy heiress, you entertain
With avocado and pink champagne

So warm, romantic and unashamed
She'll pucker up and spot those fangs
She'll do a loop
But please don't goof
Just relieve her of her handbag
And drown her in the soup!

(GENGHIS and WRAITH go to opposite wings and
collect silver toppers and canes.)

You've gotta be a connoisseur of crime –
You've gotta be a connoisseur of crime.

ALL

If you want flair – style – sophistication
Smart Alec scintillation
In your struggle to the top
You must let the others rot
If you wanna be a super-rat like me –
If you wanna be a super-rat like me.

DRACULA   Now you try, Mother.

WRAITH

I'd find a lover, who's rather rich
Then buy a cottage, beside a cliff
I'd build the bedroom, right on the edge
I've got the feeling you've seen ahead!
My man is panting and full of sport
I'll wear my nightie, naughty short
He'll do a loop
But I won't goof
I'll open up the doorway
And help him with a boot!
I wanna be a connoisseur of crime –
I wanna be a connoisseur of crime.

GENGHIS   My turn, my turn.

DRACULA   Very well, proceed.

GENGHIS

I'd take a job, at public school
Teach 'zoo and bot' to those young fools
Prepare a potion in darkest lab
They'd gather round, I'd make a grab
Pop in a pupil, dilute for taste
Tincture of tadpole and strychnine paste
They'll look aghast
But I'll just laugh

Call it 'mixed comprehensive'
And serve it to the staff.
I wanna be a connoisseur of crime -
I wanna be a connoisseur of crime.

ALL

So -
If you want style - flair - sophistication
Long-lasting jubilation
In your struggle to the top
You must let the others rot
If you wanna be a super-rat like me
If you wanna be a super-rat -
Knowing where it's always at
Be a super rat-a-tat like me
If you wanna be a super-rat like me-e-e!

(Speaking.)   That's mean.

WRAITH

Oh, my Draccy, when I see you sing and dance like
that, so many things I think you could have done.

DRACULA

Yes, Mother, but managing a delicatessen in
Karloffia is not one of them.

(GENGHIS starts to giggle and snigger uncontrol-
lably.   He is halted by a blow from DRACULA and
he cringes to floor.)

Facile fool!   Quickly, produce the ingredients for
the experiment.

GENGHIS

I have them all, Master.   All as you requested.

DRACULA

Excellent!   I shall now climb aloft to the laboratory.

MUSIC CUE 28

WRAITH

Take care, Draccy.   There must be no mistakes.

DRACULA

I never make mistakes, Mother.   Imbecile,
(To GENGHIS.)   turn on the power!

(The apparatus boils and bubbles, numerous
 objects go round and lights flash on and off.
 WRAITH and GENGHIS jump about like excited
 children on Guy Fawkes' night - oooh!   and
 aaah!)

Good. Good. See, the chemical process works
well. We have now only to add the living tissue.
Genghis, a piece of human flesh and make it lean.

WRAITH   Which way, dear?   (She thinks the 'corn'
hilarious.)

DRACULA   Mother! Frivolous frump! Be serious for a
moment. Do not interfere - this moment is vital -

GENGHIS   - is vital.   (He copies DRACULA's mannerisms.)

DRACULA   For, once formulated, the life blood substitute
gives us the power to conquer the world -

GENGHIS   - the world.

(DRACULA slowly looks down at him at foot of
tower - a 'how dare you copy' look. GENGHIS is
suitably cowed.)

DRACULA   Think of it. How could anyone stand against us,
against my army - an army that could not be
killed!

(The left palsied hand comes up. GENGHIS and
COUNTESS WRAITH suffer from the same
complaint. They hammer it back into submission.)

GENGHIS   Here, Master, is the human tissue.   (He
passes him up a human hand.)

DRACULA   How did this happen?

GENGHIS   It came off in my hand, Master. Do not chide me.
I know I am only a clumsy fool. But I try. You
have no idea how hard I try.

DRACULA   Peace! Cast the member into the solution.
(He is about to deliver a superb speech.)
For we are about to create a liquor that will
provide -

WRAITH   (interrupting and stealing the limelight)   - an
endless process of birth, procreation and death in
one microscopic drop of this supernatural liquid -

DRACULA   I was going to say that, Mother! Honestly, that's
really upset me.   (Sulky 'camp'.)

GENGHIS   Quickly, Master, pitch in the hand.

DRACULA   Very well. But I shan't forget this in a hurry.

(He pitches in the hand and as the lights change colour, the three go into a writhing and moaning group as the process takes place. Many lights flash.)

GENGHIS   Enough. Enough.

(They are all panting.)

It is done - the life blood substitute.

WRAITH   Now, at last. We can live on until we find a new victim. Try it, son! Try it!

DRACULA   (raising a can of Pepsi Cola)   For me this is the supreme moment. I will transcend the barriers of time and space.   (He pulls the metal can opener off.)

GENGHIS   Drink, Master!

WRAITH   Drink!

MUSIC CUE 29

(DRACULA drinks down a quantity of Pepsi Cola to the advertisement music and lyrics of their latest commercial. 'Lip-smackin-cool-tastin-clear-thinkin-fizz-makin-etc. but at the end, instead of the word 'Pepsi', we hear the words LIFE BLOOD. This can be pre-recorded or sung live.)

ALL   It works!

DRACULA   (passing 'Pepsi' to the others)   Each take a draught of the elixir. Feel its renewing strength pour into each fibre of your body.

(They drink and pant back to strength. A bell is heard tolling.)

WRAITH   (panicky)   Listen. Strangers call at the front iron gates.

DRACULA   Don't get over- wrought , Mother. It could be our young schoolteacher and her pretentious brats.

GENGHIS   I shall go to the castle door to meet them, Master.

DRACULA   Indeed – but first call and awaken our own pupils,
                       those fortunate women who have already become
                       my brides in life and death.

                       (We hear cries offstage of 'Master', 'We come'.)

GENGHIS   And the Zombie Men? Will they also be allowed to
                       take part in the celebrations?

                       (We hear offstage: 'Ug!' 'Umph!' Does one say:
                       'Goody!'?)

DRACULA   Of course! All shall be present. Mother, take
                       this earring which I subtly took from the girl and
                       use it to draw her to our presence – if indeed it is
                       she that calls.

WRAITH   (taking the earring and immediately going into a
                       comatose state)   I have a vision! I see a sea of
                       blood!

GENGHIS   (knowing that the next few moments will be
                       incredibly boring)   I shall make some tea.

DRACULA   No! Stay! We must know if it is the woman I
                       crave.

WRAITH   (slightly ruffled by the interruption)   I see a
                       sea of blood – and out of it – comes a girl – a
                       young, nubile creature.

DRACULA   Ahhh!

WRAITH   – A smoking crystal vapour shrouds her face.
                       Now it clears. I see a young woman of rare
                       serenity. She–is–perfect!   (Whispered.)

DRACULA)
GENGHIS }   Perfect!

DRACULA   Come, let us welcome her to my vampire empire,
                       high up on this misty hill.

WRAITH   To meet the intravenous genius,
                       Every second's a vermilion thrill!

                       MUSIC CUE 30

                       (They climb down off the North Tower, which is
                       dragged off by two ZOMBIE MEN, and COUNTESS
                       WRAITH and GENGHIS go with DRACULA to C.

A sloping platform is placed C. on which **DRACULA**
stands. He has his back to the audience as
WRAITH and **GENGHIS** take off his cloak but hold
it up in front of his body, while he is handed a
microphone and then at the end of the opening
chant – 'DRACULA ECTOPLASMIC DYNAMITE!'
– the cloak is tossed away to discover **DRACULA**
in a silver high collared catsuit plus boots. He
resembles Gary Glitter.
COUNTESS WRAITH and **GENGHIS** both sing and
dance with **DRACULA** in the number 'RHESUS
NEGATIVE ROCK AND ROLL'. Their dances
should be fairly static – but the BRIDES' will be
an aggressive 'go-go' style of dancing using both
projections of the cat-walk, while the ZOMBIES
will have a very much more 'stomp/reggae'
approach to the piece. It needs a light show or
projected images behind the dance.)

SONG: RHESUS NEGATIVE ROCK AND ROLL

(Offstage: reprise of opening song chant is sung
by BRIDES and ZOMBIES.)

Of giant strength and giant tread
He seeks a life-force from the dead
Sleeps all day, but works all night
DRACULA! ECTOPLASMIC DYNAMITE!

DRACULA   Welcome to my Vampire Empire
High up on this misty hill
Meet the intravenous genius,
Every second's a vermilion thrill!

BRIDES   (entering and moving down to catwalks L. and R.)
O Draculame
He can charm me
He can turn me on and off
You can keep your muscles
We prefer corpuscles
When we dance the Rhesus Negative Rock!

DRACULA   Welcome to my Vampire Empire
High up on this misty hill
I supply re-vivication
Simply swallow down this cochineal pill!

BRIDES | (at the same time as above)
Rhesus-Negative-a-Negative Rock
Rhesus-Negative-a-Negative Rock
Rhesus-Negative-a-Negative Rock
When we dance the
Rhesus-Negative Rock!

ZOMBIES | O Draculame
He made us barmy
He just drove us quite insane
Changed our composition
With that small incision
Now we dance the Rhesus-Negative Rock!

DRACULA | Welcome to my Vampire Empire
High up in this castle shell
I'm a lunatic lymphatic
Every brainstorm's like a bat outa hell!

BRIDES &
ZOMBIES | (at the same time as above)
Rhesus-Negative-a-Negative Rock
Rhesus-Negative-a-Negative Rock
Rhesus-Negative-a-Negative Rock
When we dance the
Rhesus-Negative Rock!

ALL | O Draculame
You don't harm me
You launch me to eternity
'Cos when we're hobnobbin'
With haemoglobin
We can dance the Rhesus-Negative Rock!

RHESUS NEGATIVE A NEGATIVE ROCK!
RHESUS NEGATIVE A NEGATIVE ROCK!
RHESUS NEGATIVE A NEGATIVE ROCK!

I MEAN
MMM! YEA!
DANCE THE RHESUS NEGATIVE ROCK!

(At end of dance the ZOMBIES and BRIDES collapse
to the ground on the word 'Rock!' DRACULA,
COUNTESS WRAITH and GENGHIS collapse at
centre of body and hang. At this point during
applause, NADIA and PUPILS are pushed on to the
stage from the wings.)

MISS NADIA   (pulling up short)   Oh!   I hope we're not
                      interrupting anything?

                      (There is a pause, then, as they slowly turn to look
                      at her, they slowly unwind upwards with the music,
                      back to original dancing positions.   During the
                      reprise, NADIA and PUPILS get caught up in the
                      spirit of the moment and join the dance in a
                      detached way.)

                      MUSIC CUE 31   REPRISE

DRACULA   Welcome to my Vampire Empire
                      High up in this castle shell
                      I'm a lunatic lymphatic
                      Every brainstorm's like a bat outa hell.

BRIDES &   (at the same time as above)
ZOMBIES   Rhesus-Negative-a-Negative Rock
                      Rhesus-Negative-a-Negative Rock
                      Rhesus-Negative-a-Negative Rock
                      When we dance the
                      Rhesus-Negative Rock.

ALL   O Draculame
                      You don't harm me
                      You launch me to eternity
                      'Cos when we're hobnobbin'
                      With haemoglobin
                      We can dance
                      The Rhesus-Negative Rock.

                      Rhesus-Negative-a-Negative Rock
                      Rhesus-Negative-a-Negative Rock
                      Rhesus-Negative-a-Negative Rock

                      I mean
                      Mmm!
                      Yea!
                      Dance the Rhesus-Negative Rock!

DRACULA   (points to NADIA and screams)   SEIZE THEM!

                      MUSIC CUE 32

                      (GENGHIS holds the CHILDREN tight, while MISS
                      NADIA is taken by the ZOMBIES and raised aloft,
                      face upwards, head D. S. and arms outstretched.

She is borne offstage in a slow ritualistic manner.
The incidental Riff music accompanies this.
NADIA is in a swoon. During the lift and carry
the BRIDES slip fangs into their mouths.)

Bear her to the bridal chamber and dress her for
our black union. And you, my beauties, will
return to help me with our new bride.

(As he cackles he holds out his hands to the
BRIDES who kiss his hands, fingers, weaving
around him they slide sinuously down the catwalks
and off the stage through the audience. A few
attempts at unsuspecting 'auditorium' throats are
made.)

Genghis!

GENGHIS   Master?

DRACULA   See to the brats also. They may serve as an hors
                   d'oeuvre before the wedding breakfast.

GENGHIS   I understand, Master. Come, pretty ones.

                   (He shepherds them down to catwalk L.)

                   Come to the chamber of Genghis and we shall see
                   if we can find any - er - unusual games to play.
                   (He produces a human hand from his pocket and
                   shows the PUPILS.)   Eh?   (He cackles.)

JULIE   (removing spectacles)   Anatomically, most
                   fascinating.

KELLY   Hey, it's a party!

                   (They both exit with GENGHIS.)

ELVIS   (out front)   Er - like - er - stay loose.
                   (Shakes his hands.)   You know what I mean?
                   (He follows them out.)

WRAITH   (moving across stage to DRACULA, pleading)
                   May I play with the children, Draccy? There are
                   little things that only a mother can give to young
                   ones - maybe they would like to play my version of
                   'Snakes and Ladders'.

DRACULA   (quietly)   Mother.

WRAITH	Or possibly a 'Beetle Drive'.
DRACULA	(louder) Mother.
WRAITH	Scrabble?
DRACULA	(shouts) Mother!
WRAITH	Draccy?
DRACULA	Forget parlour games. Go and help prepare her for the ceremony.
WRAITH	Ooo, yes. I shall enjoy doing that. (She exits muttering other titles of games: gin rummy, pontoon, etc.)
DRACULA	(solus, moving down on to the catwalk R.) So. Now I have Nadia in my power. I shall 'change her composition with a small incision'. Sweet-tasting beauty - she makes my blood burn in my veins and my heart race with thoughts of moonlight madness.
	(A bell starts to toll.)
	But all things must wait. The bell tolls three. (There is another dong, he does a Jack Benny.) Four. See the sunlight creeps over the horizon to harass my work. Even now (He changes physically.) a dreadful weariness spreads through me. I feel my bones melting into earth and my flesh crumbling to ash. So I must rest awhile until the night and healing darkness comes again. I am weakening fast. Some small revitalising tonic before the coffin calls.
	(BRIDES and ZOMBIES start to stagger behind the gauze area. They are climbing back into tombs and graves.)
	Farquarson!
	(DRACULA calls one of the ZOMBIE men who enters with a silver tray on which stands a Pepsi-Cola can. He wears huge clompy boot.)
	Farquarson, my night cap! Quickly! (He takes the can and holds it before him like a chalice of wine.) To sleep - perchance to dream!

MUSIC CUE 33

(As he swallows it down we hear recording of
'Lip-smackin-life-givin-cool-fizzing etc. LIFE
BLOOD!)

Come, Farquarson.

(He throws a tip on to the tray which the ZOMBIE
pockets.)

The daylight burns into my brain. Come. There
is no time to lose now but much to be done - later!

(They both cackle and exit U. L.
The lights fade and a projection comes up of the
interior of a dark wood. Two follow spots pick up
NICK and FATHER O'STAKE either side of stage.
They are searching for NADIA and CHILDREN.
They go through the same crossing routine that was
employed by DRACULA and GENGHIS at the
opening of Act II.)

NICK & O'STAKE	(either side of stage, calling) Miss Nadia-a-a! (They change sides.) Nadia-a-a!
NICK	(to O'STAKE) One more, I think, Father?
O'STAKE	Indeed.
NICK & O'STAKE	(both C.) NADIA-A-A-A!
NICK	Not a sign nor sound of them anywhere since early this morning.
O'STAKE	I do not like it well, Doctor. I have a terrible premonition that they have either paid a foolhardy visit to the Castle of the Black Lake or have been drawn there by the magic powers of the Countess Wraith. But here are Herr Hans and Frau Gretel, they may have something favourable to report.
NICK	Dear friends. Have you seen or heard ought of our guests? We have searched everywhere.
HANS	I am afraid not, Doctor, unt I fear ze vorst.
NICK	This is terrible. Terrible. What can be done?
GRETEL	Do not fret so, Master Nick. Hans and I haf sent the villagers and patients of our hospital to search

every nook and cranny – they may not be in ze
hands of Count Dracula but have gone merely to get
food for their journey or even to visit the church of
Father O'Stake to say their farewells. See, here
comes Herr Booze, he will have nooze.

(HERR BOOZE is very much out of condition and
puffs onto the stage.)

O'STAKE   Steady now, brother Booze. Calm yourself, and
tell us what you know carefully and in your own
words.

(BOOZE takes a very large breath and the others
help him take it. They listen intently to a series
of strange gurgles, pops and whistles intertwined
with scribble language. It is like listening to
Harpo Marx explaining a geometrical theorem.
The general theme of the action is that the
CHILDREN and NADIA have gone to the castle and
been incarcerated. The mime should be rehearsed
very carefully.)

Thank you, thank you, brother Booze. You have
done well. God bless you, my son.

(He takes a bottle of Glublick from his cassock
and passes it to him. After a pat on the head from
all, BOOZE trundles off to be met by some other
inmates of the hospital. They are gleeful and
emit words suspiciously like 'lubbly' and 'picnic'.)

As we feared, Doctor, Miss Nadia and the
children have indeed left our flock and cast
themselves unwittingly into the hands of the black
shepherd.

NICK   Then we must act both quickly and without fear.
Herr Hans and Frau Gretel, round up as many of
our friends as you can, also contact this man.

(He hands GRETEL a card. They are both very
impressed.)

He is one of my laboratory assistants and has
been working on some secret experiments I have
been conducting on the vulnerability of the
vampire. The information he gives us could be

most vital to the success of our cause. When we
have all assembled then we will march on the
castle.

HANS   Ve vill.

GRETEL   Ve vill.

(Hand business as in Act I.)

BOTH   Indeed ve vill.

MUSIC CUE 34

NICK   Father O'Stake and I will leave directly for that
accursed place - there is only one way to deal
with this fiend of hell. Father, have you the prop?

O'STAKE   (absently)   The stage prop?

NICK   No, the pit.

O'STAKE   The pit prop?

NICK   The stake!

O'STAKE   The stake. Oh, yes, indeed I have.   (He pats
his cassock.)   All is well.

NICK   Excellent. Goodbye, friends.

(They all shake hands. NICK steps forward, out
front.)

Let us hope, for Nadia, the children and our own
sakes, that we are not-too-late! Heaven only
knows what horrors are flooding through their
minds at this moment.

MUSIC CUE 35

(NICK points at the catwalk L. as the light comes
up on NADIA and the CHILDREN, and fades on
NICK. NADIA and the CHILDREN are in white
sacrificial drapes. They are in a prison.)

JULIE   Miss Naive, I think we have landed ourselves in an
alien-orientated society.

KELLY   Yea, I'm hungry, too.

ELVIS   I think we're - er - incarcerated. You know what
I mean?

MISS NADIA	I do. I do. And it is all my naive fault, children.
CHILDREN	Oh no! That's not true, Miss Nadia. Don't blame yourself.
MISS NADIA	It is true. It is. Why, if I hadn't been such a sweet, innocent, lovingly adorable, fascinatingly pure little woman, we'd be safe at home in Wyoming.
JULIE	(correcting her) Pennsylvania.
MISS NADIA	(admonished) Pennsylvania.
KELLY	Please don't blame yourself, Miss.
ELVIS	It's like - er - programmed destiny. You know what I mean?
MISS NADIA	But I do blame myself. We are simply locked up in this dungeon awaiting a fate more horrible than death because I'm so unworldly and worse, because I'm so vulnerable!

MUSIC CUE 36 (Optional number)

SONG: I'M A NICE LITTLE GIRL

(The song is sung in a small tight group, no dance but complementary body movements.)

MISS NADIA

I'm a sweet little girl, I'm a nice little girl
I'm so vulnerable
I'm a sweet little peach
Such an unstained 'teach'
I'm the creme de la creme
I'm the creme de la creme

Anyone who can be-e-e
As innocent as me-e-e
Is easy prey, night or day
For any wicked monster who should come my way.

MISS NADIA &
CHILDREN

She's a sweet little girl, she's a nice little girl
She's so vulnerable
She's a real precious stone, she's a rare
        matchless rose
She's so debasable
She's so debasable

Anyone who can be

As innocent as she
Is easy prey, night or day
For any wicked monster who should come her way

MISS NADIA   I recall my early schooldays
My department and elite days
A candy-cool confection, that's me
Not a single imperfection
In my superfine complexion
A Gina Lollobrigida, that's me
A Gina Lollobrigida, that's me

CHILDREN   (as the same time as above)
She's a sweet little girl
She's a nice little girl
She's so vulnerable
She's a sweet little peach
Such an unstained 'teach'
She's the creme de la creme
She's the creme de la creme

MISS NADIA &   Anyone who can be-e-e
CHILDREN   As innocent as me-e-e
Is easy prey, night or day
For any wicked monster who would have his way.

Yes, she's so vul - nerable.

JULIE   Miss, I am kinda scared.

MISS NADIA   Of course, you all must be.

KELLY   Do you think that Dr Nick will come to help us?

MISS NADIA   Why, I'm sure he will.

ELVIS   I've lost all sense of time. Like - er - what's
o'clock?

JULIE   Yes, Elvis, I have the same problem. Kelly, how
do you feel?

KELLY   Hungry.

ALL   Teatime!

(GENGHIS enters and with sound effects, mumbles
and curses as he unlocks an invisible door of vast
proportions. There are many bolts and chains.)

JULIE	Look out, Miss. Quasimodo is back.
MISS NADIA	Don't use Brooklyn expressions, Julie dear.
JULIE	But –
GENGHIS	(interrupting) Enough of the prattle, chatter and singing. The master requests your presence at the – banquet.
KELLY	Ooo – fab!
ELVIS	(over shoulder, out front) Ominous. You know what I mean?
GENGHIS	Silence! Come, follow me. This way.

(He exits through imaginary door and they tiptoe in opposite direction. GENGHIS spots them.)

No! This way, fools!

(He scuttles back and pushes them through door and then addresses the audience.)

You see, nobody understands me!

MUSIC CUE 37

(THE CEREMONY OF THE FANG. The CHILDREN are held by a group of the BRIDES who have entered while NADIA is held aloft and brought D.C. NADIA is lowered onto the backs of a line of kneeling BRIDES. They have formed a human altar. NADIA's head is inverted, her head towards the audience. As she is brought to this position all sing the Chant and stretch out hands to touch her, some expose fangs in an effort to subdue their frenzy. DRACULA enters and claps his hands or cracks a whip and they back off. He is dressed in the same red garb as the BRIDES. It is a huge occult houppelande.)

THE CHANT

(At very slow tempo, ZOMBIES walk at slow processional march pace. This is sung during the preparation work above.)

ZOMBIES, BRIDES & PRINCIPALS	OF GIANT STRENGTH AND GIANT TREAD HE SEEKS A LIFE FORCE FROM THE DEAD,

SLEEPS ALL DAY BUT WORKS ALL NIGHT
DRACULA - ECTOPLASMIC DYNAMITE.

WRAITH   (spoken over incidental music)
                O Dracula. Clear before whose eye
                The present, past and future lie.
                'Ere the moonlight and the evening dies
                Seize your bounty. Claim your prize.

GENGHIS   (speaking)
                O Master, skilled in magic arts and lore
                Feed us from thy ample store.
                Prince of Vampires. King of Night.
                Dracula - Ectoplasmic Dynamite.

                (A BRIDE either side rips open the top of NADIA's
                nightdress to expose neck and upper breast.
                Velcro should hold top of dress and audience should
                hear the rip. Another BRIDE has a small dish of
                blood secreted for DRACULA's bite.)

DRACULA   (speaking as he moves towards NADIA)
                Not even beauteous frippery can hide
                The marble throat of this my bride.
                One kiss, one bite, my pretty dove
                Then waken to an ecstasy of love!

                (DRACULA stoops and bites. When his head lifts
                there are the bloody marks of his fangs on
                NADIA's throat. All BRIDES and ZOMBIES sigh,
                relishing the sight of blood.
                At this moment NICK and FATHER O'STAKE enter.)

NICK   Stop! Release those children. Just in the nick
                of time.

                (The CHILDREN run to his protective arms.)

DRACULA   How dare you enter my domain uninvited. Seize
                him!

                (The BRIDES and ZOMBIES move in slow motion
                towards him.)

O'STAKE   (producing a crucifix which he holds before him)
                No further, in the name of God, I charge you.

                (All cower and burn in the shadow of the cross as
                O'STAKE crosses to the figure of NADIA.)

In Heaven's name, what evil is this? Herr Hans, come quickly. The altar cloth. Frau Gretel, please take the cross and hold these fiends at bay!

MUSIC CUE 38   (HANS and GRETEL enter.)

HANS Here, Father.   (He gives him a purple cloth.)

O'STAKE (wiping away the blood)   Pray God we are not too late.

MISS NADIA (waking)   Where am I?

NICK She's waking. Well done, O'Stake.

O'STAKE Safe, my child, safe.

MISS NADIA Nick, is that you?   (She throws out a limp hand in his direction.)

NICK Yes, my own, I am here at your side. Do not fear. I will never leave you alone again.

(All spoken and acted in the style of a 'Twenties romantic film, like Franchot Tone.)

MISS NADIA Oh, Nick, with you I feel safe.   (She rises and runs to his arms.)

DRACULA This time it would appear you have the advantage of me, Man of God and Doctor of nothing! But you cannot hold us thus, for much longer.

GRETEL For vonce you are wrong, Count Dracula. Our Doctor has discovered a weakness in your armour unt now he has the opportunity to put it to the test.

GENGHIS Weakness?

WRAITH Challenge him, Draccy.

(DRACULA is apprehensive. GENGHIS and WRAITH back behind him suspiciously.)

DRACULA What stupidity is this you talk of?

NICK Not stupidity, friend, but

(All come to attention.)

scientific experiment.

(They relax.)

During my recent research into liquids and their
cumulative effects upon the vampire,

(He hands DRACULA a card which DRACULA tears
up and throws away, but NICK is cool.)

I came, by sheer chance, upon a new solution until
this moment unknown to the world of science.
Harmless to living beings but to the – unliving! –

GENGHIS   A new solution?

HANS   Zey shake.

WRAITH   What does he mean?

GRETEL   Unt tremble.

DRACULA   Tell me of this strange liquid. Speak. I fear nought.

NICK   You fear nothing, Count? Then tell me what you
                 think of this. Quickly, my friends!

                 (The HOSPITAL INMATES all run in. They brandish
                 bottles of Glublick. NICK pours some into his hand
                 and throws it at DRACULA. All VAMPIRES and
                 ZOMBIES scream and writhe on the ground as
                 INMATES flick Glublick over them.)

DRACULA   (hands raised in abject terror)   No! It is impossible!

GENGHIS   Help me!

BRIDES, ZOMBIES Master, we are dying!

WRAITH   What is it, my son? It burns my flesh.

DRACULA   It is – Aqua Glublictus!

                 (VAMPIRES and ZOMBIES scream.)

NICK   Precisely. Aqua Glublictus! Like fools we had the
                 answer to your evil in our very hands that night you
                 called at the inn of Herr Hans and Frau Gretel.
                 Glublick! And now we shall use it as we should have
                 done that evening. Destroy them!

ALL   Glublick!

                 MUSIC CUE 39

                 (The INMATES move in amongst the BRIDES and

ZOMBIES. As they spray them with Glublick, they
groan, scream and spin off the playing area or
crawl across floor to wings. The attention of the
INMATES now grouped R. turns to DRACULA but
especially to WRAITH and GENGHIS now. They
start to slide away from DRACULA as two
INMATES proceed to open trap in readiness.)

GENGHIS   Don't look at us that way.

WRAITH   We are sensitive.

GENGHIS   Why are you - standing - by the trap-door to the
                lower vaults?

WRAITH   Draccy, help me! I'm your mother!

DRACULA   I know.   (He does not move.)

NICK   You cannot escape your doom, infamous creatures.

O'STAKE   Quickly, the trap-door. Clod, revenge yourself
                with the Church's blessing.

                (The trap-door opens - green fumes pour out.
                COUNTESS WRAITH and GENGHIS back towards
                it.)

GENGHIS   No, not the Black Lake.

WRAITH   Draccy, save me!

                (They enter the trap, arms waving in the smoke.)

GENGHIS   I am drowning in its murky depths!

WRAITH   The weeds are pulling me under!

BOTH   AAIEEOOUU!

                (They disappear below level of the stage but trap
                remains open.)

DRACULA   So! You have sacrificed their bodies to the green
                slime of the lake swamp.

                (Both GENGHIS and COUNTESS WRAITH appear
                suddenly again for one second up and down with
                another 'AIEOOUU!')

                Is this the fate you intend for me?

O'STAKE   No, Count Dracula. We know you have no fear of that inky hell.

NICK   There is only one sure way to end your reign of
                terror.

GRETEL   Hold him fast!   (Signals to the INMATES to
                hold DRACULA fast.)

DRACULA   No! No! Not the stake!

                (They hold him and he is held above the gaping
                trap. The fumes change to red and a blood
                container is placed below the trap out of vision of
                the audience. GRETEL brings a hammer or
                mallet to FATHER O'STAKE while HANS holds a
                huge stake above DRACULA's body.)

O'STAKE   Yes, Count Dracula. The stake. And may God
                have mercy on your black and evil soul!

                (The stake appears to be hammered through the
                body. It is, in fact, hammered down into deep
                blood container and comes up dripping.
                DRACULA screams as the stake is driven in.)

DRACULA   COME DEATH THAT I MAY SLEEP AND BE
                FREE-E-E-E!

                (They let the body drop onto the safety platform
                below and we hear a recording of a long scream as
                the body drops down a great height followed by a
                delayed splash and bubbling noises.)

MISS NADIA   Oh, Nick. It's horrible. Horrible.

                MUSIC CUE 40

NICK   Don't look, my love. Your eyes should only
                behold images of beauty.

GRETEL   He is right, my dear. Come. Stand back from zis
                accursed place unt forget vat you haf seen unt
                heard.

HANS   Jah. Vise vords, vise vords. My littel apple-
                dumpling speaks vise vords.

MISS NADIA   You mean I must try to erase from my memory all
                the horrors and torments I have experienced?

O'STAKE   Yes, my child.

JULIE	Problematic!
KELLY	Difficult!
ELVIS	Indelibly imprinted – you know what I mean?
O'STAKE	But it must be so. This abomination is over and we should leave this dark place.
HANS	Jah. Leave as quickly as possible.
GRETEL	I shall prepare rooms for everyone at the Brauhaus. For tonight ve shall sleep ze sleep of peace unt contentment – the loathsome Count Dracula is no more and the sun will shine again in Karloffia.
NICK	You speak with the tongue of poetry and beauty, my dear Frau Gretel. Yes, the nightmare is over and all men can now be free. We shall return to the inn.
MISS NADIA	May I thank you, Father, Hans, Gretel – (Looks at NICK.) everyone. But before we return I should like to be – alone – with Nick for a short space.
	(There is a pause as NICK and NADIA are locked in an enamoured stare.)
HANS	(breaking the silence) Of course! Of course! Ze magic of Aphrodite flies through ze evening air – eh, Gretel? (He nudges her and speaks to NICK and NADIA.) You must have a few moments privacy – zat is certain.
O'STAKE	Indeed. Come all. We have much to do and later I think I shall be called upon to arrange a small 'celebration'. Do you not think so, Frau Gretel? (With a knowing wink.)
GRETEL	Jah. Jah. (Laughing.) Come, everyone, to ze inn.
	(All exit except CHILDREN. They are staring at the entranced couple.)
	Come, Hans. (As she exits.) Hans, who iz zis Aphrodynamite you are talkink of?

HANS

Aphrodite.   (Spelling it out.)   Aphro-D-I-T-E, my love. Do not concern yourself - I love only you, my honey-bunch.

(They exit. There is a pause. FATHER O'STAKE pokes his head back in from wing and in an urgent whisper.)

O'STAKE

Children! Come quickly! There are three birds too many still in the nest.

(The CHILDREN realise and the gawping stops.)

JULIE

(out front)   Sensual enrapture!

KELLY

(out front)   Love-hunger.

ELVIS

(out front)   Sloppy stuff! You know what I mean?

(They exit with FATHER O'STAKE.)

NICK

Oh, Nadia, at last we are alone and all evil is behind us. In the brief moments we have been together I have learned to live!

MISS NADIA

And you have taught me, Nick, that there is not only horror in the world but love also. And that real 'amour'   (Her French pronunciation is dreadful.)   can overcome all malevolence.

NICK

My own,   (He breaks D.R.)   this is difficult for me to say - but - as you may know, I have recently been carrying out some experimental research into physical and emotional sensations. (He hands her one of his cards.)

MISS NADIA

(impressed as she reads it)   Oh!

NICK

This work is of supreme importance and has many demands and I shall need a great deal of help. So I wondered if you could consider - that is, whether you feel you could -

MISS NADIA

(interrupting and holding out her hands)   Yes, Nick. Yes. I will be your scientific assistant.

MUSIC CUE 41

NICK

(embracing her)   Nadia! Now we can truly fulfil a new destiny, loving and being loved. Together we shall spread compassion throughout the galaxies!

(They move onto the catwalk R. while PRETTY GIRLS move onto catwalk L. or C. Both groups are spotted in 'sci-fi' light. Clouds scud across the gauze. The song is a dreadful send-up but should be sung sincerely.)

SONG: STARRY SPHERES

(PRETTY GIRLS hum the tune.)

NICK	Ho-o-ld my hand
MISS NADIA	(speaking) Baby, you know that I will
NICK	And we shall climb
MISS NADIA	(speaking) I'll follow you anywhere
NICK	Beyond the sun
MISS NADIA	(speaking) Beyond the moon
TOGETHER	Beyond the frontiers of the Starry Spheres We two We two Together.

(PRETTY GIRLS ooo the tune.)

MISS NADIA	Ta-a-ake my heart
NICK	(speaking) Baby, I'm a prisoner of love
MISS NADIA	And we shall soar
NICK	(speaking) Point me to the sky
MISS NADIA	High above life
NICK	(speaking) Fly through the night
TOGETHER	To drink the nectar from the Vaults of Time We two We two Together.

(PRETTY GIRLS aaah serenade as from score underneath spoken dialogue.)

NICK	(speaking) O Nadia You know, that I know, that you know, We can take flight

Gently blow on the wings of our love
So let us fly in the blue crystal of the morning
With neither rest nor respite
Towards the paradise of our dreams.

ALL   (singing)
We two
We two
Together.

(PRETTY GIRLS aah serenade as musical score under spoken dialogue.)

MISS NADIA   (speaking)   O Nick
I know, that you know, that I know
Look, my eyes are on fire
My heart blazes with the heat of your love
All I ever dreamt of has come to pass
Now others will only stand and gasp
Aghast, seeing nothing can surpass
True hearts - at last!

ALL   We two
We two
Together.

Ho-o-old my hand
And we shall climb
Beyond the sun
Beyond the frontiers of the Starry Spheres
Beyond the frontiers of the Starry Spheres.

NICK   Come, Nadia, our friends are waiting to welcome us.

MISS NADIA   Yes, we must see them all and tell them the divine news - before we start our life together.

NICK   Nadia. There is just one other small thing.

MISS NADIA   Yes, Nick, of course - anything.   (Concerned.)

NICK   You forgot to return my card.

(She does so.)

MISS NADIA   Oh!

NICK   Thank you. Come, they are waiting for us.

(During the dialogue, the 'BRAUHAUS' sign is

dropped and tables set by the INMATES. They
form a tight group at one of the tables set at an
angle L. At the centre table standing and sitting
are FATHER O'STAKE, GRETEL, BOOZE and
CLOD and the CHILDREN. HANS stands on the
table. Secreted on the table is a white cloth,
candlesticks, eight white hymn books, a white
vestment and a Bible. The INMATES have a box
under their table which contains confetti. These
things should be hidden and disguised as much as
possible from the view of the audience.)

HANS   I see them. Here they come.

GRETEL   Velcome home, Nick and Nadia.

O'STAKE   God bless you both and welcome.

                (INMATES and CHILDREN echo the welcome.)

NICK   It is truly refreshing to be safe here in your happy
                inn.

MISS NADIA   And truly refreshing to be safe from the Evil One.

KELLY   You can say that again.

MISS NADIA   And truly refreshing to be safe from the Evil One.

NICK   (interrupting)   Nadia. I think Herr Hans has
                something he would like to say.

MISS NADIA   Yes, of course. Herr Hans, you are looking very
                important standing up there on the table.

GRETEL   (to the others, confidentially)   It vill be one of
                his poems. Specially written for ze occasion.

ALL   Bravo! A poem! Let us hear it, Herr Hans!

HANS   (importantly taking out an incredibly small piece of
                paper and putting on a huge pair of spectacles)
                A poem unt a toast written by Herr Hans and read
                by –

ALL   HERR HANS!   (They cheer.)

HANS   Jah! Exactly so. Unt now, quiet, please.

                (There are many hushes and fingers to mouths.
                HERR HANS speaks slowly, carefully and with
                poetic feeling.)

Now ve are hopeful of peace unt content
Ve've vitnessed ze end of zat black malcontent
So raise up your glasses, unt drink vun down quick
A toast to our heroes, young Nadia unt Nick.

(There is a pause.)

GRETEL   Zat is it?

HANS   (with pride)   Zat-is-it.

(Another pause.)

GRETEL   (speaking slowly, with affection)   It is a
beautiful poem. Not long, my pumpernickel, but
ze best you haf ever written.

(They applaud ecstatically. It is an old
Karloffian custom to applaud poetry no matter how
poorly done, as long as it is written sincerely.
The applause breaks into the singing of the poem.
During the song, the INMATES sway at the tables
while during the chorus, O'STAKE, NICK, NADIA,
the CHILDREN, HANS and GRETEL, CLOD and
BOOZE form a circle C. and dance a stamp and
hand slapping Austrian dance.)

MUSIC CUE 42

SONG: LUBBLY GLUBLICK   REPRISE

HANS   Now ve are hopeful of peace unt content
Ve've vitnessed ze end of zat black malcontent
So raise up your glasses, unt drink vun down quick
A toast to our heroes, young Nadia unt Nick!

ALL   Drink Lubbly Glublick
Fill up your glass to the brim
Drink Lubbly Glublick
Till it o'erflows the rim
All your troubles will stop
You'll find peace in each drop
When Glublick goes fizz, ping and pop!

GLUBLICK!

MISS NADIA   What a marvellous ending to such an adventurous
day.

NICK   But not quite the end, Nadia. Shall we tell our

friends the good news?

O'STAKE	You do not need to tell us, Dr Nick. We can guess the news you have for us, for is that not just the suspicion of a blush on young Nadia's fair cheek?
MISS NADIA	(hands to face, and out front) Oh, my heavens! Does it show?
O'STAKE	It does indeed, my child, and, if my guess is right, then you have named the day?
NICK	We have, good Father, and the time of our betrothal will be this very night - if you would be so kind as to carry out the ceremony?
O'STAKE	I would let no other priest have the honour, my son. Dear friends all, our young doctor and the lovely teacher are to be wed - tonight!
	(There are many cheers and congratulations; the INMATES consume more Glublick than is good for them.)
GRETEL	Oh, congratulations, my dear. I know zat you vill be very 'appy togezzer.
HANS	Jah. As happy as Gretel and I haf been zese forty years. (He nudges her playfully.)
GRETEL	(blushing to the roots, coyly) Oh, Hans!
HANS	Oh, jah! And haf no worries for the children. Ve shall see zat zey arrive safely home on ze next Transylvanian flight to Amerinka.
CHILDREN	(as in opening scene routine, out front) WOW!
MISS NADIA	Thank you both kindly, dear Hans and Gretel. This is a secret I have always kept to myself but now I can speak openly. I was an orphan child and lived most of my early years alone and uncared for, but now I can truly say I have found a real mother and father of my own.
CHILDREN	(as in opening routine, out front) YUK!
NICK	Come, Father, the wedding. We shall be wed tonight, Nadia, travel to Heidelberg in the morning and after a short honeymoon, return to

	our university studies. (He hands her a card.)
MISS NADIA	Oh, Nick. I - love - you.

MUSIC CUE 43

(The central table is quickly covered by a white
cloth, candlesticks are placed either end which
LOOBY ignites. The INMATES form a choir
behind FATHER O'STAKE who puts on a white
gown and holds a large Bible standing behind the
table/altar. During the singing, the INMATES,
one by one, take off their operating theatre caps,
holding their hymn books. The CHILDREN form
one side of a V-shape leading to the altar, while
HANS, GRETEL and BOOZE form the other.
NICK and NADIA walk towards the altar slowly in
a pavan-processional manner. They sing the song
underneath FATHER O'STAKE's ceremony.)

SONG: TWO PATHS, BE ONE

| CHORUS | Let these two live in love's warm embrace
Bless them and keep them in happiness safe
Better for worse, for wealthy, for poor
May they be rich from the love that they store. |
|---|---|
| | Let these two walk in peace evermore
Bless them and keep them in safety so sure
Make their way clear, to walk in the sun
May her way be his way, two paths, be one. |
	(Repeat sotto voce)
	Let these two live in love's warm embrace -
	(The ceremony commences.)
O'STAKE	Nick and Nadia. You have decided to be joined
together here in Karloffia according to the old
promises and customs that have been in use for
hundreds of years. The ceremony is simple but
lasting as your love and pledge should be.
Do you, Nick, love Nadia - truly?
NICK	I truly do.
O'STAKE	And do you, Nadia, love Nick - truly?
MISS NADIA	I truly do.

O'STAKE   Then, Nick and Nadia, in as much as you have
                 sworn that you love each other 'truly' and have
                 witnessed publicly to that truth, I now pronounce
                 that you are no longer two but one in our sight and
                 your love.

                 (NADIA and NICK turn. We hear wedding bells as
                 the INMATES, HANS, GRETEL and the CHILDREN
                 throw confetti over the couple. After just a few
                 seconds of festive celebration there is a sudden
                 wedding photograph freeze. During this the choir
                 hums a reprise of 'Two Paths Be One' as FATHER
                 O'STAKE moves away from the freeze and comes
                 D.S. to catwalk L. He addresses the audience
                 with an epilogue over the top of the humming choir.)

                 Since the first night we opened up our theatre door
                 We've done our best - the best can do no more
                 So, dear friends, off to your blessed homes of
                            peace
                 Once entered there, your quarrels all must cease.
                 And as for vampires and those lakes of black
                 There are no such things!
                 So sleep you well at that.
                 This loving couple will need our special care
                 So think on them, and in their fortunes share.

                 (The group fractures as NICK and NADIA come
                 forward to FATHER O'STAKE, the INMATES
                 strike the two tables and stay in the wings as
                 HANS, GRETEL and the CHILDREN move to a
                 group dressing D.R.)

NICK   Father, thank you for your help and kind words.

MISS NADIA   Thank you, dear Father.

O'STAKE   It is one of my duties to join together loving
                 couples but this was more a pleasure than a duty.
                 May you always have joy together.

HANS   May your home never be cold. Quick, Gretel,
                 the presents.   (He nudges her.)

GRETEL   (she shyly produces two huge hot water bottles -
                 exact replicas of the bottles we saw earlier in the
                 play)   From Hans and I from our hearts to your

	toes. May zay alvays be varm and tender. Vas zat right, Hans?
HANS	Nearly - almost nearly, my love bird.
	(They laugh.)
JULIE	(removing glasses, very serious as always) Miss Nadia, may you realise everlasting bliss and happiness in your marriage.
KELLY	Yes. Say - I hope you can cook, Miss.
ELVIS	Like - er - cool vibrations. You know what I mean?
O'STAKE	I think they know what you mean, Elvis. But come, you must dally here no longer, but be off and start your new life together. Coachman! Take their bags.
	(A dark figure, face muffled up, picks up the bags and moves to U.C. and stays there.)
HANS & GRETEL	Goodbye, unt God bless!
	(NICK and NADIA move and stand beside dark figure. NICK centre of the three. They wave as they go.)
CHILDREN	We'll see you in the summer vacation next year. Bye! Take care!
O'STAKE	Well, don't just stand there. Off with you, and safe journey.
NICK	Of course. (He turns to COACHMAN.) Come, let me help you with these bags, they are -
	MUSIC CUE 44
	(The COACHMAN throws off hat and muffler to one side. It is DRACULA re-incarnated.)
	No! No! It's not possible! (He is horror-struck.)
DRACULA	On the contrary, my friend, it is very possible. (As he cackles, he reveals fangs.)
NICK	In Heaven's name - (He turns to NADIA.)

Nadia, do not be afraid. I will protect you yet
again.

MISS NADIA   (smiles, revealing fangs)   Will you, darling?
                    I think I shall like that.

                    (NICK is dragged off by NADIA and DRACULA.)

NICK   No! No! You f-i-e-n-d-s!

                    (There are screams, cackles and flashing lights.
                    Both DRACULA and NADIA move slowly to his
                    throat in a tight spot as HANS, GRETEL,
                    O'STAKE and the CHILDREN who have covered
                    their faces and cowered up to this point start to
                    move off with the three PRINCIPALS. The
                    CHORUS reprise offstage the song 'Dracula
                    Spectacula Show!' During this, DRACULA takes
                    off cloak in the wings and returns to C. with
                    GENGHIS and COUNTESS WRAITH either side of
                    him. The BRIDES move onstage to catwalks as the
                    others slide off in preparation for reprise of
                    'Rhesus Negative Rock'.)

                    MUSIC CUE 45

                    SONG: THE DRACULA SPECTACULA SHOW
                                                        REPRISE

                    BATS! SCREECH! BLOOD! RITES'.
                    You'll need the exorcise
                    WHITE! FANGS! EYES! ICE!
                    Do not trust that smile.

                    So if your cuppa tea
                    Could be Christopher Lee
                    Then fly with us tonight
                    'Cos it's a two-way trip
                    In a cataleptic fit.
                    Watch out in case he bites!

                    (By this point BRIDES and ZOMBIES are
                    assembled on catwalks L. and R. and DRACULA
                    is U.C. in glitter suit with re-incarnated
                    GENGHIS and COUNTESS WRAITH to left and right
                    of him. DRACULA had his glitter suit below the
                    long cloak.)

MUSIC CUE 46

(transpose to REPRISE)

SONG: RHESUS NEGATIVE ROCK

DRACULA

Welcome to my Vampire Empire
High up in this castle shell
I'm a lunatic lymphatic
Every brainstorm's like a bat outa hell!

BRIDES)
GENGHIS)
WRAITH)
NICK & NADIA)

(at the same time as above)
Rhesus Negative-a-Negative Rock
Rhesus Negative-a-Negative Rock
Rhesus Negative-a-Negative Rock
When we dance the
Rhesus Negative Rock!

ALL

O Draculame
You don't harm me
You launch me to eternity
'Cos when we're hobnobbin'
With haemoglobin
We can dance the Rhesus Negative Rock!

RHESUS-NEGATIVE-A-NEGATIVE ROCK!
RHESUS-NEGATIVE-A-NEGATIVE ROCK!
RHESUS-NEGATIVE-A-NEGATIVE ROCK!

I mean –
MM!
YEA!
DANCE THE RHESUS-NEGATIVE-ROCK!

MUSIC CUE 47

(At the end of song they freeze looking at the
audience, until band plays 'Come Fly Transylvanian
Airways'. This is sung R. by the PRETTY GIRLS
and is used for the curtain call. The BRIDES and
ZOMBIES bow and exit, INMATES and OTHERS
likewise. During their bows the PRINCIPALS
form the following group U.C.:

WRAITH DRACULA NADIA NICK (BRIDE 1)
GRETEL HANS (BRIDE 2) GENGHIS O'STAKE
          JULIE   ELVIS   KELLY

After CHORUS bows the first named characters in

the following pairs run across the stage and grab
in lecherous fashion, the second named character.
They exit as a couple to screams, giggles and
obvious delight – off to the woods!

ELVIS	takes	JULIE	(off R.)
HANS	takes	BRIDE 2	(off R.)
NICK	takes	WRAITH	(off R.)
GENGHIS	takes	KELLY	(off L.)
O'STAKE	takes	GRETEL	(off L.)
DRACULA	looks at NADIA but then		
	grabs	BRIDE 1	(off L.)

leaving NADIA alone C. She is now in a tight
spot, she looks off, at the audience. She is livid,
stamps her foot.

BLACKOUT

MUSIC CUE 48

(The band plays audience out with 'Starry Spheres'
sung by PRETTY GIRLS still on catwalk R.)